THIS BOOK BELONGS TO:

Barbara Rice

©IF13103

THREE CONSORT QUEENS

Three
Consort Queens

ADELAIDE, ALEXANDRA & MARY

Geoffrey Wakeford

ROBERT HALE · LONDON

ISBN 0 7091 2017 6

Robert Hale & Company
63 Old Brompton Road
London S.W.7

PRINTED IN GREAT BRITAIN BY
EBENEZER BAYLIS AND SON LIMITED
THE TRINITY PRESS, WORCESTER, AND LONDON

For
DIDY AND AMELIA

Contents

Illustrations

ILLUSTRATIONS

PICTURE CREDITS

National Portrait Gallery: 1, 2, 4, 5; Radio Times Hulton Picture Library: 3, 8, 9, 10, 11, 12, 13, 14, 18, 19, 20, 21; The Mansell Collection: 6; The Press Association: 7; Bassano and Vandyk Studios: 15, 16; Associated Press: 17.

Foreword

QUEEN DOWAGERS are a relatively modern substructure of the British monarchy. This book synthesizes the lives of the three who in the past century and a half, after serving as queens, lived on to support their husbands' successors in the public work which has increased with the growth of democracy: Queen Adelaide, the consort of William IV; Queen Alexandra, the consort of Edward VII; and Queen Mary, the consort of George V.

Thirty Years a Queen, published in 1968, showed how Queen Elizabeth the Queen Mother preserved and strengthened the image of the 'family' monarchy. But the guidelines were fashioned and secured by her three predecessors. The British people have appeared on the whole to flourish under queens regnant, and the activities of kings have tended to obscure the influence of queen consorts. Yet in the shadows cast by the throne it is possible to discern the essential contributions made by these three queens to the stability of the Crown.

Between Adelaide and Alexandra the incomparable Queen Victoria flourished in solitary grandeur. There were times after the death of the Prince Consort when Victoria sighed for release; and the king who preceded her, and the two who succeeded her, were more than once deflected from abdication not merely by an innate sense of duty but by the sympathetic and unfailing support of their consorts. The mystique of Victoria permeated the lives of all three Queens. Yet Adelaide, the meek and guileless German Princess, was the true foundress of 'Victorianism' when she reformed the Court, as well as her husband, after the profligacy of George IV and his so-called 'wicked' brothers. Alexandra restored gaiety to a Court which for nearly sixty-four years had been repressed by the prudish solemnities of the Victorian era.

Queen Mary, the most cultured of the three consorts, went on to develop the concept of the 'working Queen', refreshing the monarchy with a stimulating mixture of conservatism and progressiveness.

There had been no queen dowager in this sense until the death of William IV in 1837. Between the Norman Conquest and the accession of William and Adelaide twenty of England's thirty-seven queen consorts (including the less fortunate of Henry VIII's wives) died before their husbands. Six remarried. Four were divorced. Catherine Parr, the sixth wife of Henry VIII, briefly survived the King, but in that short interval took as her fourth and last husband Thomas, Lord Seymour of Studeley. She therefore cannot be listed among the queen dowagers. Nor can her two dowager successors in the seventeenth century. Henrietta Maria lived on for twenty years after the execution of Charles I, partly as an exile in her native France; but her life at Somerset House after the Restoration has attracted scant attention from historians, probably because it was overcast by the 'permissiveness' of her son's Court. The last of the queen dowagers before Adelaide was Henrietta Maria's daughter-in-law, Catherine of Braganza, the widow of Charles II; but after the King's death she retired to Portugal, having failed to secure the Stuart Succession, and was heard of no more.

Only in modern times has the queen dowager been expected not to marry again. Adelaide was young enough, 45 at the King's death. But she sincerely loved William, and the alleged love affair with her favourite courtier, Earl Howe, owes more to imagination than to fact, as does the friendship of Queen Alexandra and Oliver Montagu. It was Adelaide's bitter experience to lose the infant daughter who might have reigned as Queen Elizabeth II. The tragedy could have driven a wedge between her and the King; instead it bound them more closely.

No ordinary woman can imagine herself in the position of a princess faced with queenship: the several biographers of Adelaide, Alexandra and Mary find common ground when they describe the reluctance of all three to step into the fierce light which beats upon the throne, the most exalted in the world. Adelaide was almost resigned to lifelong spinsterhood, and even after marriage her husband was only second in the succession behind the Duke of York. Alexandra's expectation of the English crown was almost destroyed by her own and her husband's grave illnesses and by a near assassination. Up to her early twenties Mary, a 'poor relation' of the Royal Family, had little reason to believe her destiny to be linked with the House of Saxe-Coburg and Gotha. But when they ascended the throne all three reacted similarly: the King was the King and in broad matters of policy they must subordinate self, consciously and whole-heartedly, to the service of the monarchy. All suffered in varying degrees for and through their kings, probably more than biographers will ever be able to discover. Certainly in the case of Queen Alexandra the destruction of her private correspondence has removed for ever a source of enlightenment on which it is attractive but unrewarding to speculate.

Ill health precluded Adelaide from any notable exertions as queen dowager, but half her income and much of her time was dedicated to charitable causes. Alexandra worked almost to the end and distributed largesse with even greater prodigality. Mary, a victim of parental extravagance, was sparing of her wealth but gave unstinted service to the community in war as in peace; and in old age as in youth she worked probably harder than her predecessors and suffered personal trials far more agonizing than theirs. Yet she outlived them. Adelaide died at 57 and Alexandra at 80. Thanks to her 'Cambridge constitution' and her refusal to relax, Queen Mary survived to the age of 85 into her granddaughter's reign after an intimate connection with four British sovereigns and an heir to the throne who all died in her lifetime.

Of each of these graceful ladies it can be written with Homer that she moved like a goddess and looked a queen. They were certainly not as other women.

Queen Adelaide

I

The Awful Philippic

In March 1837 Queen Adelaide retired to her chamber with yet another of her colds. She was a martyr to chills, an affliction shared with the Duke of Wellington; but the present attack proved more than usually severe and left her prostrate. By the time she felt able to face the *beau monde* again a series of three misfortunes befell her.

The first was a call to the deathbed of her mother, the Dowager Grand Duchess of Saxe-Coburg-Meiningen. While the Queen was in Germany her favourite step-daughter Sophia, the eldest of the King's massive illegitimate brood, died at Kensington Palace. Life at William IV's Court had been enlivened, and the King's wavering sanity rebalanced, by Sophia's mordant wit, usually exercised at the expense of the Holland House Set, of whom her father had once declared that he would as lief admit the Devil to his table as a Whig Minister. Now Sophia was dead after childbirth in her middle forties. The shock drove a dagger into William's paternal heart. He began to die of grief. He was 72.

Sophia had married the first Baron de L'Isle and Dudley. She died on 10th April, a few weeks after George IV's discarded morganatic Roman Catholic wife, Maria Fitzherbert. After the mourning for his daughter, William, with Adelaide, drove from Windsor to St. James's Palace on 17th May for a series of public engagements. At the last of these, on the 19th, William fell in with some old shipmates, to whom he discoursed with more volubility than logic upon the relative merits of the battles of La Hogue and Trafalgar. It was an unwise subject, but unwiser still was the vehemence with which he embarked upon it. He over-taxed his strength. Next day, back at Windsor, he felt too unwell to eat. Laudanum was administered, but asthma, the old enemy, had struck again. William sank into a wheelchair, then into his bed, where his numerous bastards droned around him uselessly under their stepmother's compassionate eye.

These FitzClarences, all ten of them, had been the fruit of the King's good-natured liaison with the actress Mrs Dorothea Jordan, but she had died in lonely squalor in Paris twenty-one years earlier after having devoted two decades of her life to the comforts of her royal bedmate at Petersham and then at Bushey Park. All but one of the ten—Henry, who died in India in 1817 after an undistinguished military career—were filially named after the sons and daughters of their reluctant grandfather, King George III. Although William was an ever-tender parent, an overwhelming if belated sense of public and private duty enabled him to discard his mistress without much display of grief when, in 1818, he was called upon to find a bride with whom he might legally secure the succession. His choice fell upon the German princess Adelaide. She was younger by nine years than the youngest of George III's fifteen children, twenty-seven years William's junior, and the same age as Sophia FitzClarence.

Adelaide was 25 when she timorously intoned her marriage vows and undertook to shepherd William's unruly flock, half of whom were under 17 and all of whom were inclined to romp. The task of managing an irregular and turbulent household would have driven her beyond endurance but for her failure, as a foreigner, to understand them; what she did not understand she did not grieve over. She was impenetrably calm. Her natural kindness and love of other people's children—for she was con-demned to bear babies but not to rear them—overcame the natural repugnance of the young FitzClarences to their father's lawful wife. The eldest, George Augustus Frederick, even came to regard his stepmother as "the best and most charming woman in the world". George was not the most grateful of sons; he badgered his parent for more money than he could afford and sulked himself into an estrangement. Sire and son were reconciled by Adelaide, always the peacemaker, always the diplomat, after William had reminded his first-born of his own 'double duty' as king and father. One of William's first acts as king was to confer the Earldom of Munster upon George, and subsequently Queen Victoria made him her *aide de camp*. Neither act of royal grace deflected Munster from suicide before he was 50.

In sum William had done very well by his 'boys', providing them with nearly £30,000 apiece besides their annual allowances. But they were rarely satisfied. The fifth son, Lord Augustus FitzClarence, abused his father because he had advanced a Mr. Wood in the Church instead of promoting his own son. The Reverend Lord Augustus, brooding in his rectory at Mapledurham in Oxfordshire, refused to perform the marriage ceremony of a FitzClarence sister under their father's roof. It was a mean and petty revenge. But now at the end, reunited with the dying King, Augustus padded quietly about the sick chamber, lips quivering with silent prayers, hands raised in silent appeal to the King of Kings. Each day he read the Morning Prayer to his father. The eldest surviving daughter, Lady Mary Fox, hardly left the patient's side. Such dedication was heart-rending. The Queen had been sorely tried by her stepchildren, but their penitence impressed her and she thanked God for it. She made nothing of the fact that during the last ten days of his life she herself slept in her clothes. But, then, she loved him. William never spoke of death in her presence. The faded hero of Reform wished to live another ten years for the sake of the country. When this ideal seemed unattainable he replaced it with an *idée fixe*: he must survive until his niece Victoria had passed her eighteenth birthday, else her unscrupulous and detested mother, the Coburg widow of his brother the Duke of Kent, would reign as Regent. Adelaide trembled every time her husband hoarsely invoked damnation on 'that woman', for it upset his stomach whenever he thought of her.

She could not forget 'the awful philippic' of the previous August. Ah, that terrible day! It was the climax of a sustained campaign of effrontery, designed by the Duchess to stamp her image on Society as the mother of the future queen and the power behind the throne. Her signal deficiency in charm churned her regal brother-in-law into a foul temper at the sight of her, although he was usually all sweetness towards little Victoria. Sometimes he simulated deafness, and stampeded the Duchess on social occasions by pretending to hear nothing she said. Relations began to worsen when the Duchess flounced around the countryside showing Victoria to the people—*her* people. These preposterous 'progresses' turned the King's animosity into positive hatred of his sister-in-law. Moreover, was it seemly that she should be seen pouring her domestic woes into the receptive ear of Lord Durham, an implacable Reformer and son-in-law of the Whig statesman Grey? Matters came to a head in August 1836 when the Duchess ignored Queen Adelaide's birthday on the 13th. She and the princess had been invited to Windsor to celebrate both this and the King's birthday on the 21st, as well as to attend the marriage of William's fourth daughter Augusta to her second husband, Lord John Frederick Gordon, on the 24th. But the Duchess also had a birthday to keep at this time, and she would keep it at Claremont, come what may. Meanwhile, behind the King's back, she had occupied against his express orders a suite of seventeen apartments at Kensington Palace, enough for a regiment. When the King discovered this "unwarrantable liberty" the Duchess had already snubbed the Queen. It was too much.

At dinner on the eve of his birthday William sat next to the Duchess, with Victoria facing him. His health was toasted. Then, like a volcano erupting, he poured upon the Duchess the red hot lava of his discontent, calling on God to spare him for another nine months to avoid a Regency. Should God oblige, then the royal authority would smoothly pass to Victoria and not—here the blood rushed to his head—to "a person, now near me, who is surrounded by evil advisers and who is herself incompetent to act with propriety in the station in which she would be placed". The King considered that he had been grossly and continually insulted by "that person", and he was determined no longer to endure a course of behaviour so disrespectful. William went on to complain about the manner in which "that young lady has been kept away from my Court" and repeatedly from his drawing rooms. "I would have her know that I am King," he said, fixing a bloodshot eye upon Victoria, "and that I am determined to make my authority respected; and for the future I shall insist and command that the princess do upon all occasions appear at my Court, as it is her duty to do." Victoria had by this time melted in tears, her mother was ablaze with indignation, and Adelaide was so deeply distressed as to be bereft of speech.

"Come, Victoria!" the Duchess ordered, sweeping her frightened daughter out of the room, while through the shocked silence

William could be heard muttering under his breath: "That woman is a damned nuisance, damned nuisance, damned nuisance."

During his last days William lay bepillowed on his golden bed. He said goodbye to his brothers Cumberland and Sussex and to all his surviving children. Thereafter he refused to sign paper or give audience. Most of his utterances appeared to lack sense. But he survived to see his niece reach the age at which she could reign without a Regent. That hurdle overcome, he then yearned to live long enough to mark the approaching anniversary of Waterloo. A Dr. Chambers, insinuated into the castle because the Queen had so little faith in the King's own doctor, Sir Henry Halford, was enjoined by William to "try if you cannot tinker me up to last over it". Even twenty-two years after the battle the old admiral was liable to burst into encomiums of Wellington, and he often quoted Castlereagh's parliamentary account of the victory, ending with the memorable words: "The British and French soldiers, after the action, washed their bloodstained hands in the same stream and from opposite banks congratulated one another on their courage."

Waterloo Day came and the dying Sovereign whispered, "God bless the Duke of Wellington!" and fondled his banner. Now, he declared, he was ready to meet his Maker before sunset the following day, 19th June. When Chambers assured him without much conviction that he might see many sunsets yet the King in his repetitious way sighed, "Oh, that's quite another matter, another matter, another matter." Augustus glided mournfully in the wake of the Archbishop of Canterbury as the Primate approached to read the Visitation of the Sick for the last time. Adelaide knelt beside William, made the responses and helped him turn over the pages of his prayer-book. The Archbishop pronounced the blessing; she burst into tears. "Bear up, bear up!" came the King's voice. They were almost his last words. Augustus, not the most reliable witness, bent down and distinctly heard his renegade father breathe, "The Church! The Church!" The King's head rested upon Adelaide's shoulder, his hand in hers. The Queen supported him with her other arm. Thus he died between two and three of the morning on 20th June 1837.

So Victoria was Queen, the Duchess of Kent was Queen Mother by courtesy, and Adelaide in her forty-fifth year was

Dowager Queen. But for the grace of God her own daughter Elizabeth would have reigned. Elizabeth had been born just before Christmas 1820 when Adelaide was Duchess of Clarence. Her baptismal names were Elizabeth Georgina Adelaide, and she would have ascended the throne as Queen Elizabeth II, possibly with Adelaide as Regent. But she was born six weeks too early, weighed far too much—11 pounds—and nearly killed her little mother in the process. Death came painfully to the baby princess during a convulsion brought on by an entanglement of the bowels. She survived only a month. A white marble effigy of the princess rested in an alcove at the castle.

Now, bereft of husband, children and such power as she had exercised, Adelaide was alone in the world. All she had was the frozen likeness of Elizabeth and the dead King, and over these she wept bitter tears. On 10th July the King was entombed in the royal vault at Windsor, while she watched the last rites from the closet in St. George's Chapel. She had poured out her full heart upon him despite the disparity in their ages.

Within three years England had been deprived of two potential queens regnant. The death of George IV's only legitimate heir, Princess Charlotte, at Claremont in 1817 had led to the great race among the eligible younger sons of George III to shed their paramours, contract regular marriages, and produce heirs to the Crown of St. Edward. If the poor mad King should have no legal grandchild the throne must pass to a German cousin, the Duke of Brunswick; he was then 15 but appeared to be even more eccentric than his Aunt Caroline, the estranged wife of George IV. The choice of brides open to the virile Hanoverians was more or less restricted to Protestant Germany.

It was a distressing situation. Rarely had so much depended upon the use of gynaecological instruments. The princess toiled in labour for nearly fifty hours. In their dilemma her doctors hesitated to use forceps, even when it was obvious that the future King of England was in deadly peril; by the time they reached a decision it was too late. The birth was three weeks overdue and the boy, who weighed 9 pounds, was born dead. Charlotte accepted the blow philosophically. She was plied with wine to induce sleep and forgetfulness. "They have made me tipsy!" she told the faithful Stockmar, her Coburg husband Leopold's *fidus Achates*. A little later, with a loud cry of, "Stocky! Stocky!" she passed beyond criticism, five hours after her dead baby, on whose sex the Stock Exchange had wagered considerable sums. The tragedy staggered England, and Charlotte's leading man-midwife, Sir Richard Croft, afterwards shot himself when he lost another mother in childbed.

Charlotte died at 20. Her reprobate father, gouty and obese, proclaimed through the Court Circular: "As it is the will of Divine Providence, His Royal Highness is in duty bound to submit to the decree of Heaven." There is some evidence that Croft desired to perform a Caesarian section, but the Regent was exchanging pleasantries with his mistress Lady Hertford in Suffolk and could not be reached in time to give his assent. Charlotte, with her fair tresses and slightly bulging blue eyes, was no more. Only memories remained. Her ill-matched parents had grappled squalidly for her custody and her affection. For a time the Regent had hidden her from Queen Caroline at Warwick House, but the child fled in a hired post-chaise to her mother at Connaught Place. Escapades of this kind, together with a visit to Weymouth when she insisted on hauling herself up the side of a warship on a rope ladder, plus the alleged cruelty of her grandmother Queen Charlotte towards her, conspired to make her the most popular member of the Hanoverian dynasty. Popularity in such circumstances was not hard to achieve. The nation rejoiced when, after having twice rejected the Prince of Orange ('Slender Billy'), she fell into the arms of Leopold of Saxe-Coburg. For that "best of all husbands" she is said to have nurtured "an amount of love the greatness of which can only be compared with the National Debt". The Surrey estate of Claremont, built for Clive of India, had been a wedding present from the British government.

The tragedy of Claremont was Adelaide's opportunity, if it may be so expressed, for the family into which she married suffered from the defects of its virtues and the tittle-tattle of gossips like Burney, Creevey and Greville. Ladies-in-waiting who keep diaries are ever to be feared and distrusted in Court circles, and Fanny Burney wrote much about George III's grievous disorder which might better have been left to the imagination. The old monarch's pathetic delusions, his conviction that he was the Elector of Hanover, his revived passion for the love of his youth, Lady Pembroke, were heightened by the scribblers; and

there was a general belief that he was possessed by the Devil.
Yet who could say the Sovereign was mad when, on opening
Parliament after one of his recoveries, he began his speech with
the interesting formula, "My Lords and Peacocks"? The Commons at any rate had been described by epithets less euphemistic
but scarcely more apt.

When Adelaide married William the old blind King was in a
padded apartment at Windsor, but his austere Queen was very
much herself. Charlotte was a lady of the utmost German prudence
and virtue, a matriarch of Lutheran strictness, who, having
failed to inspire affection in her inharmonious offspring, lived to
endure their disloyalty. Royal history has occasionally produced
dull, plain and worthy queen consorts, but Charlotte excelled
them all in the dull, plain merit of her effort to "preserve society
upon a respectable footing". The King was a sober blade before
his mind clouded over. A leg of mutton and his wife, as the rhyme
claimed, were the chief comforts of his life.

A dozen of their fifteen children survived to welcome Adelaide
to England in 1818. Of those the most lurid, the most condemned,
was the Prince Regent. A crust of Creeveyism has hardened over
the man beneath the corsets so that it is almost impossible to
resurrect his virtues. But had he been as infamous as some historians have asserted, a nation which had destroyed Napoleon
could easily have disposed of the lesser enemy at home, had be
been an enemy and had they wished. But they apparently did not
wish. Even in the year after Peterloo the Cato Street plotters
failed to murder the Cabinet and carry off the heads of Sidmouth,
Wellington and Castlereagh in sacks. The people preferred devils
they knew to republicans they did not. For all his faults fat George
was more interesting than Thomas Creevey with his "sharp
birdlike little eye for the oddities of human conduct", from which
he invariably excluded his own. No crumb ever fell from the
Regent's table at the Brighton Pavilion but that the sparrowish
Thos. nimbly retrieved it in transit to the floor, and by some
process of moral alchemy transformed it into a morsel to be
regurgitated over and over again at country house parties. Everybody knew of the Regent's delusion that he had commanded the
Xth Hussars at Waterloo—"Your Royal Highness's memory is
better than mine," said Wellington. But 'Diddy', as his stepdaughters called Creevey, in reporting what Wellington is

supposed to have said after Waterloo, garbled the facts. This had not deprived him of his esteemed place in history as the chronicler of 'Prinney' and his Court. Lampoonists dubbed Creevey 'Old Grey Pantaloons', possibly because through his wife he was a connection of Lord Grey. He was also connected with the Molyneux of Lancaster, being the natural son of the first Earl of Sefton. In one way and another he had admirable opportunities to cultivate a talent for the invention of uncorroborated testimony.

Yet even Creevey could not have invented Queen Caroline. The Regent had been parted from his flamboyant wife for twenty years when Adelaide sailed to England. Adelaide had heard her undivorceable future sister-in-law described as 'the mad princess', for in the year before she left Germany the gallivanting Queen and her lover Bergami had appeared at Karlsruhe in strange Turkish costumes; and she had embarrassed the Grand Duke of Baden by donning the garb of an Oberlander peasant, with a huge headdress, flying ribbons and glittering spangles. At Baden she also rode horseback with a pumpkin on her head, explaining that nothing kept her so cool in the hot weather. The Regent's contribution to English life was said to have been the acquisition of old masters and new mistresses. One of the latter was Lady Jersey, who did her feline best to wreck the Prince's marriage to Caroline. This was not difficult. The Brunswick princess talked much and washed little. Her knowledge of English fashion was rudimentary, and Lady Jersey induced her to clad her rakish figure in the most ridiculous garments, claiming that George would like them; but George was even more embarrassed than the Grand Duke of Baden. The mistress accompanied the royal couple on their honeymoon, hovering like a witch over the marriage-bed. The birth of Princess Charlotte provided her father with an excuse to get rid of the mother. Caroline cast around for means of revenge. Wax models of royal personages were popular in those days. Queen Charlotte had one of the Regent as a baby. From her Caroline conceived the idea of modelling the Regent, then much larger and somewhat less appealing. She proceeded to embellish the model with a pair of horns. It was then her pleasure to stick pins in the finished product, to relieve her feelings. As their ill-fated daughter afterwards remarked: "She would not have become as bad . . . if my father had not been infinitely worse."

One day in 1821 Castlereagh told George IV that his mortal

enemy had died. "What! is it possible that she is dead?" he asked, hope rising in his breast. But Castlereagh meant Napoleon. The Queen, barred from throne and Coronation, despite popular sympathy and the legal exertions of Brougham, died soon afterwards at Brandenburg House, Blackheath. In the early morning of her death a boat passed down the river, filled with some of those religious sectaries who had taken a peculiar interest in her fate. "They were praying for her, and singing hymns, as they rowed by," Lady Charlotte Bury recalled. "At the same moment a mighty rush of wind blew open the doors and windows of the queen's apartment, just as the breath was going out of her body. It impressed those who were present with a sense of awe and added to the solemnity of the scene." Such was the ill-used predecessor of Queen Adelaide. Yet however harsh his conduct towards his wife, the Regent revealed only the better side of his volatile nature to Adelaide; and he shed bitter tears when her daughter Elizabeth died.

George IV's next brother Frederick—'the brave old Duke of York'—was 54 at the death of Princess Charlotte. For more years than he cared to recall, Frederick had been married to the Prussian niece of Frederick the Great, but he and the Duchess Frederica found their greatest pleasure in living apart. Even that arrangement was preferable to what might have been: originally he was expected to mate with Caroline of Brunswick. Frederica buried herself in a Surrey grotto, lavishing affection on a collection of forty pet dogs and a variety of monkeys and tropical fowl. Her talents as a hostess were reinforced by an ability to stay awake all night and sleep all day in the grotto. On her death the Duke nobly refused to remarry, not because he loved his wife but because he could not make the Duchess of Rutland his wife.

No one who upheld the monarchy wished the throne to go to the younger Dukes of Cumberland and Sussex. The former, generally regarded as the wickedest of Victoria's uncles, was King of Hanover. He had been in wedlock for two years to his cousin Princess Frederica of Solms-Braunfels when Adelaide joined the Royal Family. This Frederica was a lady of doubtful virtue and of even more doubtful judgment, for she was credited with the murder of an earlier spouse and, having married Cumberland, sadly disappointed the hopes of his father's subjects in England and his own in Hanover by failing to slay him, too. Sussex had two children by Lady Augusta Murray, but they were barred from the throne by the Royal Marriage Act. Sussex, the most liberal-minded of the family, refused to marry during Lady Augusta's lifetime. York's other younger brothers were persuaded without much hardship to surrender their attachments and seek permanent brides of the blood royal. Edward, Duke of Kent, gave up his admirable Madame de St. Laurent—the 'old French lady'—and, with a loan of £1,000 from the Czar of Russia to defray expenses, travelled to Baden to review princesses. A Spanish gipsy had fore-told that he would sire a great queen, so he went about his work with zest, especially as he had authority to take a wife for £12,000 down and £30,000 a year. In this way he secured the hand of Victoria, daughter of the reigning Duke of Saxe-Coburg-Saalfeld and widow of Emich, Prince of Leiningen, with results that were to satisfy the needs of the monarchy for as far ahead as could be seen. The youngest brother Adolphus, Duke of Cambridge, also issued forth upon a reconnaissance in depth among the Rhineland beauties. First he chose a bride for William; the Princess Augusta of Hesse-Cassel. But he fell in love with her and, with William's blessing, married her. This decision too, was to have a profound influence on the royal line.

William, next in the succession after York and before Kent, had proved himself fecund beyond the dreams of constitutionalists. The production of little FitzClarences had become a major industry, occupying much of his mature life. Now he was called upon to make a more acceptable contribution to the security of the realm by sacrificing Mrs Jordan, whose underwear was sold to defray her funeral expenses in Paris. At first he found potential queens hard to come by, but after a rebuff here and a delicate refusal there, which might have blunted the resolution of a less ardent wooer, he finally settled for the Princess Amelia Adelaide Louisa Thérèse Caroline, eldest child of George, Duke of Saxe-Coburg-Meiningen, and Louisa Eleanora of Hohenloe-Langenburg. The princess, who took her second name from a German queen of the tenth century, was less than half his age. Adelaide was a lady of homely qualities, not a great beauty or personality; but goodness of heart was written in her sweet expression. William, whose ego was perhaps his most treasured possession, hoped she would not be 'dazzled' by the match, although all the honour might seem to have been conferred from the other side.

Marriage into a family whose male members usually sought out women as unlike their royal mother as possible was a formidable undertaking for a shy and inexperienced foreign princess. Adelaide, her brother Bernard Eric and her sister Ida had been brought up in the pocket-handkerchief state of Meiningen while the armies of Napoleon and Alexander I clanked across Europe and back again. When Adelaide was born on 13th August 1792 the French Revolution had begun to "betray the hopes of philosophers". Waterloo was fought when she was 22. Meanwhile, she had seen little Meiningen occupied in turn by the Grand Armée and the ragged hordes of Russia. Louisa Eleanora, a widow of immense moral courage and commonsense, refused to evacuate the ducal castle at Altenstein, and by 1813 had managed to preserve the duchy for her son. Her husband George had died when Adelaide was 11 years of age. The punctilio of his régime contrasted with his liberal political leanings. One of the first to benefit from the Duke's democracy was his mother. On her death he had her buried not in the family vaults but in the public graveyard because he deemed her "worthy to lie among her subjects". He also made the People godparents of his son and gave Bernard Eric the third name of Freund. Liberal thinkers found refuge in Meiningen when they had sufficiently exasperated the reactionary rulers of their home states. Schiller repaid the Duke's hospitality by praising him publicly, if faintly, as a bore of considerable ability—the dramatist of Enlightenment was an authority on bores.

2

Marriage to William

WEALTH, beauty, achievement. Without those advantages Adelaide had been contemplating cheerfully a lifelong spinsterhood. In 1816 the younger Ida married first. Her bridegroom, the gargantuan Duke Bernard of Saxe-Coburg, stood 4 inches above 6 feet. He was described by Sophia Brownlow, afterwards Adelaide's Lady of the Bedchamber, as a "sort of Brobdignag Cupid". From Lady Brownlow—how those ladies-in-waiting worked at their diaries!—comes an equally vivid description of the conditions under which Adelaide and Ida lived at Altenstein. A bedroom with a common floor and "not a scrap of carpet". On each side a small bed with calico curtains. Two small tables and a few light chairs. 'Comfortless' it was, to outsiders; and the Earl of Erroll, who married a FitzClarence, considered it "a doghole that an English housemaid would think it a hardship to sleep in". As no English housemaid had ever seen it, this opinion is neither here nor there.

Less prejudiced sources suggest that the little girls spent a happy childhood beneath the ducal roof, feeding on old stories of the Thuringian forest, retailed to them before a crackling log fire by their old nurse as she knitted away with chilblained fingers under the pale gold ray of oil lamps. The castle itself was cosy rather than comfortless during the long, hard winters when for weeks the family and their retainers might be snowed up among the frozen pines. There is a suspiciously neat legend that Adelaide's favourite fairy tale was *The Beauty and the Beast*, and that she dreamed of marrying a wicked prince whom she could reform; unlike Ida, who could have been happy with any boar-hunting young landgrave or elector from the *Almanac de Gotha* and, indeed, was. The story seems to have been invented after it was known which beast Adelaide was to marry. A young German princess of no outstanding qualities except innate good breeding might well feel honoured to marry a son of the King of England and a brother of the King of Hanover. If she felt any qualms about the 'wickedness' of her elderly bridegroom she never expressed them. Naturally, she stood in awe of William, who drank and swore like a navvy, comported himself like a buffoon, and was seriously considered by the Russian ambassador's wife to be mad —"the least educated of all the English princes . . . no knowledge, vulgar English habits and manners . . . his conversation also vulgar".

There had been love affairs enough. At Kew he had embraced the attractive daughter of his German tutor. Queen Charlotte turned a blind eye to the attachment; it "keeps William out of mischief". Womanizing and drinking bouts between long sea voyages as an officer in the Royal Navy had helped to widen the breach between William and his prosaic parents. Once he brought home from the West Indies a coloured girl improbably named Wowski, whose capacity for self-effacement earned her the sobriquet of 'Wowski the Mole'. Another early love was a maiden of 16, Miss Fortescue, and but for the 'iniquitous' Royal Marriage Act he would have married her. Two years before the death of Princess Charlotte the prince had contemplated marriage with Princess Sophia of Gloucester, but her mother was a commoner and he decided against it: William might be a rake, but he knew where to draw the line. The Princess of Dannemark, on the contrary, turned him down because she could not bear the FitzClarences or even the thought of them; not many women could have been blamed for refusing to mother a large and unpredictable second-hand family. Then the rich Miss Tylney-Long, when William approached her, flew terrified into the rescuing arms of a rival swain more her own age. Finally there was Miss Wykeham, the heiress of Wenman, an Amazon who flexed the biceps and refreshed the tissues by galloping large-boned horses over five-barred gates with great frequency and power. The Regent and his mother jointly slew this unsuitable passion.

England's future William IV was the third son of a royal family which is generally considered to have been the last to 'live like kings'. He was born on 21st August 1765, christened William Henry by Archbishop Secker of Canterbury, inadequately educated at Kew, and destined for some honours but more disappointments in the Navy, that 'glorious' and 'noble' profession, as George III called it. The proud father radiated nothing but affection towards "my young sailor", but ordered that he was to be shown not the "smallest marks of parade". Soon he was a midshipman, and in this modest office helped to relieve Gibraltar in 1780, when he was noticed favourably by a visiting grandee, Don Juan de Langara. "Well does Great Britain merit the empire of the sea", rhapsodized the don, "when the humblest stations in her Navy are supported by princes of the blood." Two years later William narrowly escaped kidnap by one of George Washington's agents in New York, but it was there, too, that he first met Nelson and became his staunch admirer, a fact which disperses some spurious arguments that William was no real judge of men. As early as 1787, eighteen years before Trafalgar, the prince was so devoted to the future admiral that he gave away the bride when Nelson married the widow Frances Nesbit in the West Indies. "In every respect, both as a man and as a prince, I love him," Nelson wrote to his brother. Nelson's loyalty to William is said to have distorted his assessment of his true nature. But how could Horatio have known that he himself would be extinct by 1805 and his royal friend King in 1830? In fact, Nelson had no illusions about William's chief defect as a naval officer: he was a martinet. Presumably the Lords of the Admiralty agreed. Although, or perhaps because, William had been promoted to rear admiral by the time of the French war, he was rejected for active service against Napoleon's fleet.

The Prince was created Duke of Clarence in 1789, the year of the Bastille, having threatened his father that unless he received a dukedom he would stand for the Commons as prospective Member for Totnes. The King chose the lesser evil and granted Letters Patent. Shortly before this had begun his association with Mrs. Jordan, to whom he allowed £1,000 a year. As she was contributing seven times as much to the common pot, this was not an over-generous contribution to the housekeeping expenses at Bushey, where the amiable mistress begat his ten children in fifteen years. William brought up the young FitzClarences with "tender affection". But he was lacking in a sense of occasion. He orated in the Lords on the wickedness of adultery, denouncing the adulterer as "an insidious and designing villain who would ever be held in disgrace and abhorrence by an enlightened and civilized society". It mattered little to him that his bigamously-inclined brothers were listening open-mouthed. The rambling and sometimes incoherent nature of his public remarks earned for him the nickname of 'Silly Billy', which he shared with the Duke of Gloucester, his sister Mary's unhinged husband. Most of his spontaneous speeches were said to have been "gifts by regular instalments to all who wished his father's children ill", although he rose to Demosthenic heights on the death of Nelson. He opposed Wilberforce's anti-slavery campaign. 'The whites", he proclaimed, "must keep up adequate numbers of themselves, of the strictest military discipline and headlong courage." They must maintain constant watchfulness against arming the Negroes, expel every roaming missionary from Africa, and immerse the blacks "in illiterate stupidity". William's genius for talking apparent nonsense incensed the diarist Greville, who thought his morbid official activity indicated incipient insanity. The morbid unofficial activity of Greville was not noticed until his diaries were published after his death, when Victoria almost exploded with wrath.

All William's peccant idiosyncrasies, whether rumoured or actual, were mercifully concealed from Adelaide. The courtiers of St. James's made rough jokes about the Duke of Clarence. His head was described as being of the shape of a pineapple, although there were statesmen with heads like marrows who had done the country infinitely more harm. Adelaide was never wooed, for Clarence was far too busy to fetch his bride from Meiningen. Money was his greater preoccupation, not without reason. He owed £56,000 and had ten children to keep. His brother Kent had laid siege to the robust charms of the widowed Prince Leopold's widowed sister Victoria, after having first cast off his 'old French lady'. For this act of grace Edward received another £6,000 a year. He had asked for more, but parliaments are so unreasonable provided other ways are open to them of squandering the public funds. Clarence wanted £20,000 cash on the barrel and at least £40,000 a year to marry Adelaide, instead of the £18,000 he was getting. When Castlereagh amended the asking figure to £10,000 a year he was told that the question was "not what it might please the Duke of Clarence to take, but what it might please the people to give him". In the end his income was increased by £6,000. The least predatory of George III's sons, the Duke of Cambridge, also received an extra £6,000, but Cumberland got nothing.

Negotiations for the hand of Princess Adelaide had meanwhile opened with the Duchess of Saxe-Meiningen through Freiherr von Konitz. Throughout these sensitive exchanges the envoys of the most influential nation in the world acted as though the princess were the huntress and the Duke of Clarence the quarry. They were in fact trying to exact a higher price from the British government in this mercenary charade, and the feelings of Adelaide and her mother were not spared. At one stage the overtures were suspended. William threatened to make do with mistresses, but the Regent and Queen Charlotte appealed to his competitive sense. Were his more or less virginal younger brothers Kent and Cambridge alone to replenish and refresh the succession when he, the father of ten children, had exhibited such exceptional signs of potency? William's pride was touched. The *pour parlers* resumed. On 19th April 1818 he and Adelaide were formally betrothed. Adelaide's dowry was settled at 20,000 florins, with 5 per cent interest, payable while she remained a wife and not a mother. If she bore children she would receive 5,000 florins a year. Meiningen was to provide pin-money of 6,000 florins a year. William was to defray household expenses and also give Adelaide £2,000 a year, to be raised to £3,000 should he advance in the line of succession.

As a sailor the Duke of Clarence felt a little adrift on the seas of matrimony. He clutched at the anchor of his self-respect to the end, making it plain and loud, from parlour to poop deck, that in marrying Adelaide, whom he had never met, he was offering hostages to fortune from a deep sense of duty to his king and his country. Adelaide, he afterwards discovered when he found the time to inspect her, was not only rather slight but also somewhat plain, with flaxen hair and a meek and amiable disposition, no ambition, no yearning for the limelight, and no demands on anyone. Yet the Duke was a substantial catch, in her mother's view. Was it not better to be the daughter-in-law and sister-in-law of kings—even perhaps Queen of England one day—than to moulder in Meiningen as the sister and the aunt

3

of solemn German dukes and duchesses? So ran the thoughts of
the Grand Duchess as she hurried her apprehensive daughter to
the ship on a voyage to the throne. All was ready—except the
bridegroom.

Adelaide had received the most felicitous letters of welcome
from her future mother-in-law, from the Duchess of York
(despite all the canine distractions at Weybridge) and not least
from William's sisters. At this time two of the original six were
married but childless and one was destined neither to wed nor to
bear. The other two were regrettably unmarried but not childless;
like certain princesses of Spain, it was said of George III's girls
that unless they were married off early the heir was likely to
arrive before the husband. However, married or unmarried, they
all sympathized with Adelaide and, if they were not all to prove
loving and considerate sisters-in-law, for the present they showed
her more marks of affection than their portly brother. William
had, indeed, demonstrated more chivalry towards Louis XVIII,
finding it no hardship or inconvenience to accompany the
restored Bourbon to France in 1814. But a voyage to the Continent to meet his bride four years later hardly merited his serious
contemplation.

Thus when the travellers from Meiningen stepped uncertainly
upon English soil after an arduous cross-Channel passage of eight
hours, no William impatiently paced the quay at Deal. Cavalry and
infantry made a hot, brave show in July streets bright with bunting,
and ships off-shore hoisted flags and boomed joyful cannonades.
But not one of the King's large family turned up. The two ladies
and their attendants proceeded to London, spreading the uneventful journey over two days. Preposterously, to rate it no less, the
Duke of Clarence was out of town when Louisa and Adelaide
reached their base at Grillon's hotel in Albermarle Street. Only
William's eldest bastard awaited them there. George Augustus
Frederick was some two years younger than his future stepmother,
and if his presence was an affront to her she did not show it.
Presumably the fault lay not wholly with William. Constitutionally
the Regent, acting for his father, must meet Adelaide first. In due
course his ornate magnificence was announced. The flustered
bridegroom arrived at ten o'clock that night. He was fat and
53. As true love had as yet had no chance to mellow her judgment,
he impressed her as a middle-aged, corpulent, compulsive

talker with the manners of a bumpkin, and her heart sank.

The Regent, fervently desiring William's marriage, was relieved and reassured by Adelaide's modest appearance. It was all so unlike the scene all those years ago when his emissary the Earl of Malmesbury had presented to him Caroline of Brunswick, whom he had not previously seen. "Harris, I am not well," said the Prince on that famous occasion. "Pray get me a glass of brandy." Malmesbury tactlessly offered him a glass of water and George stamped out with an oath while Caroline exclaimed, "Mein Gott! Is zat ze Prince? He is large, coarse and by no means like his portrait." The first meeting of William and Adelaide, on the contrary, while it was certainly not love at first sight, produced no mutual antagonism. William came to love and cherish Adelaide, and, on the whole, this partnership, like so many other arranged marriages, succeeded tolerably well. While Adelaide lacked the matronly virtues and the beauty of Mrs. Jordan, William was by no means the Beast of her dreams. If the cause of England was to be served Adelaide would have to make the best of it. But first she was to face an even more exacting ordeal. She must visit her future mother-in-law.

Queen Charlotte was ailing, but she was still cold and hard. She had withered under the burden of her husband's malaise, and her roistering sons and repressed daughters were small comfort to her in her old age. Adelaide's first meeting with Charlotte was less disagreeable than she had anticipated. The old Queen hailed the young princess as an ally in a long vain struggle to support William upon the tightrope of public duty. After kissing hands Adelaide toured London, embraced relations and friends of the Royal Family, and smiled and curtsied at receptions. A grand banquet was given in her honour at Carlton House, where the Coldstream Guards' band blustered in the conservatory and the Regent was at his most condescending. But wherever she went Adelaide was struck by the unpopularity of her fiancé and his brothers. The remorseless rhymes of the former doctor John Wolcot who called himself Peter Pindar denounced William's 'desertion' of Mrs. Jordan—"After you'd got her money, too, Which she so freely gave to you", adroitly interpreting public contempt for the 'race for an heir', for the allowances demanded by the King's sons on marriage fell on the taxpayer, adding to the burden of post-war economic distress. Two days before William and Adelaide were betrothed, his sister Elizabeth at the impressionable age of 48 had married the Landgrave of Hesse-Homburg, whose imperfect grasp of the subtleties of the King's English diverted Queen Charlotte at the wedding ceremony. Public prints described the bridal pair as 'The Two Royal Humbugs'. They were enormously stout. The Landgrave rarely took a bath, a process which because of his girth he found both unconvincing and inconvenient. When two months later the Duke of Cambridge married his Hessian love Augusta the news-sheets proclaimed: "More Humbugs, or Another Attack on John Bull's Purse".

The only feasible reply to these attacks was a prudent demonstration of economy. A modest double ceremony was arranged at Kew. Two pairs were to be married for the price of one: Clarence and Adelaide shoulder to shoulder with Kent and Victoria. A crisis in Charlotte's health necessitated a two days' postponement, but at last the marriages were solemnized on 13th July before an improvised altar in the Queen's drawing-room in the presence of the Archbishop of Canterbury, who pronounced them men and wives with Lords Sidmouth and Liverpool as witnesses. The Regent, with invincible largesse, gave away both brides, Adelaide in silver tissue, Victoria Mary Louisa in gold. The Queen was led back to her apartments and the wedding breakfast proceeded. William devoured large quantities of venison and was the life and soul of the party, made a pretty speech (as he sometimes could when he had prepared what he was going to say) and maintained a gallantry towards his bride in gratifying contrast from his previous behaviour. He was affability itself to his new sister-in-law, the Duchess of Kent: their estrangement was a long way off. Tea was taken near the pagoda in Kew Gardens, and the Clarences drove off in their spanking new chariot to the Duke's apartments in St. James's Palace. The unfortunate Mrs. Jordan was forgotten, and her disconsolate orphans moped at Bushey.

As Adelaide stood on the balcony in the rain for an hour that night, showing herself to the crowd in St. James's, she wondered what the future held for her in a country, now moving into the industrial era, where the chasm between rich and poor was almost unfathomable. Already she had begun to tremble for the future of monarchy in Europe. All but three of Adelaide's twenty-five years had been obscured if not actually menaced by war. A whole generation in England had never known peace. Accordingly statesmen in their obsession with Napoleon had neglected social problems. But soon these burst into the glare of daylight with a vehemence of volcanic force. In the year of Adelaide's marriage felons were treated almost with savagery. Sheep stealers, coiners, forgers and burglars were gibbeted publicly in batches. Pest holes like the prison at Ilford rang with the shrieks of prisoners who were blistered as a torture. In the same jail prisoners crouched because they could not stand up under the crushing weight of their chains. Women with suckling infants were condemned to solitary confinement on a diet of bread and water. The horrors of the Fleet and other debtor prisons were realities which probably even the dynamic prose of Dickens never fully exposed. Snipe could be shot in Tyburnia, but another half a mile away could be found some stinking corpse-strewn canal, and beyond that the verminous hovels of Seven Dials and the overcrowding of Portman Square, where a small court of twenty-four houses sheltered 700 Irish. The East End festered with disease. In George's Yard, Whitechapel, 2,000 people were crammed into forty houses. People drowned their miseries in drink. Typhus and cholera killed thousands who did not succumb to starvation or alcohol. Women of 30 often looked like old crones of eighty.

The metropolis compressed all this squalor into a relatively small compass, but large and numerous pockets of wretchedness prevailed throughout a land where it was deemed economic to pay Dorset labourers 8s. a week, Manchester cardroom operatives between 8s. and 12s. a week, and Yorkshire labourers 12s. to 15s. a week—when a loaf of bread cost 1s. 9d. The war had promoted mechanization, and the introduction of machines brought fresh misfortunes. 'Ghost' villages were created by the wholesale desertion of people to the towns. Ricks were fired, threshing and weaving machines hacked to pieces by hungry labourers, who blamed them for their troubles, and Ministers lived in the shadow of assassination. Loafers and prostitutes jostled around Clarence House, which the Duke and Adelaide were eventually to make their London home. The Duke of York was accosted and abused in the avenue leading to St. James's Park. Marshalmen were brought in to restore respectability to the neighbourhood. But there were no police. Watchmen vainly tried to keep the peace.

Troops were brought in when the civil authorities panicked, as they frequently did, notably at Peterloo.

At the top of the social register was a royal family whose titular head, now in an advanced stage of porphyria, was still blamed for the disasters of the American rebellion. Rarely had the outlook for the British monarchy been bleaker, with Europe convulsed and affairs at home in chaos. Yet in all the turmoil £90,000 could be lavished on transforming the red-brick Buckingham House (where William was born) into a stone palace, designed by Nash for George IV, as were so many other unnecessary royal residences. Pall Mall, where rags and riches touched, had just been equipped with the new gas lamps. Already along this thoroughfare Adelaide, as she planned her honeymoon, heard the revolutionary tramp of iron-tipped heels.

Twenty-four hours after the nuptials the Grand Duchess left for Meiningen. In her state of bridal euphoria Adelaide felt no loneliness; in any case, she was soon to spend a whole year in Germany, a consummation which reflected not only William's consideration for his bride but also his relative lack of funds. Meanwhile the Duchess of Clarence tripped gaily into a whirligig of amusements, banquets, receptions and other jolly-making. William feasted and made love to his little *gemutlich* princess in a four-poster bed at St. James's, and it dawned upon his royal grace that he was the lucky partner. Surprisingly he was the first to reform in an age of Reform. No woman seems to have seduced him after his marriage. Away went the celebrated *polisson* manner; the celebrated opsimath became "quiet and well-behaved like anybody else". The taming of the shaggy old coxcomb of the Mayfair salons was attributed to his demure wife. The Fitz-Clarences in the main were disarmed by her friendliness and, after the shock of their father's perfidy towards their Thespian mother, came to regard Adelaide as an elder sister. The little Duchess reorganized the family home at Bushey, to ensure the comfort of the three youngest motherless girls, and then ordered the coachman to drive her to Kew. She felt grateful to the old Queen and wished to express her thanks before she left for Germany, for she was irked by a premonition that she would never see Charlotte again. The Queen talked pleasantly enough, but of everything but herself and her health. Adelaide's only reward was to be told that "you will do William good", and she was dismissed with a gracious nod. As the door closed she felt misgiving, returned to the room, and through the door took one last peep at her in-domitable mother-in-law sitting up stiffly in her bed. Charlotte heard the door creak and called Adelaide back to her bedside. The two women embraced briefly. In old age Charlotte looked even uglier than when she discovered early in her married life that the English people did not warm to her because she was "not pretty". Her phaeton-driving king in his happier days had over-turned her in a field, and the broken nose resulting from the spill had not improved the Mecklenburg profile. But Adelaide loved the 'unlovable' Queen, and her heart sank as she bowed out of the dying presence. She felt that she had embraced a tombstone.

A few days later the Duke and Duchess of Clarence were in Hanover, where the Duke of Cambridge since his marriage had been reigning as Viceroy. The faithful citizens, united to Britain since the reign of George I, mustered in strength to welcome the Viceroy's brother and his wife. Two months later Adelaide found herself pregnant concurrently with Augusta, the young Duchess of Cambridge. On 19th March 1819 Augusta delivered a bonny boy, who as George Cambridge was to grow up to sire a bevy of morganatic FitzGeorges almost as troublesome to him as the FitzClarences had been to his Uncle William, and to command the British Army and fiercely resist the changeover from scarlet tunics to khaki. When Augusta began labour, William, although he had almost renounced alcoholic beverages, was trying to pour some courage into his younger brother when he was called to Adelaide's bedside. Her doctors had begun industriously to bleed her, with the consequence that on the same day as Augusta she gave birth, but prematurely, to a daughter. Charlotte Augusta Louisa, named for her paternal grandmother, her aunt and her maternal grandmother, lived seven hours. She was buried in the castle next to George I. For ten days Adelaide lived in a trance of pain and grief. "I trust this amiable little dutchess [sic] will soon recover her strength," wrote William's eldest sister Charlotte, a lady of alarming obesity who herself had suffered loss in childbed and was to die without issue as Queen of Württemberg. "By all accounts she is the very woman calculated to suit my dear William's taste, and he loves her very much." The disappointment made William ill. But the tragedy drew him and Adelaide even more closely together. They genuinely rejoiced when the future

Queen Victoria imperiously entered the world at Kensington Palace on 24th May, "a pretty little princess as plump as a partridge". The two cousins, George of Cambridge and Victoria of Kent, were to share many of the joys and vicissitudes of the nineteenth century, except, of course, mutual pleasure in George's renegade marriage. The 'race for an heir' was close-run indeed when, three days after Victoria's birth, Frederica in Berlin presented the wall-eyed Duke of Cumberland with a son, another Prince George.

Within three months William was writing enthusiastically to Lord Liverpool that there was "every reason to believe the Dutchess once more with child". He would arrive at St. James's with "this excellent and admirable Princess" on 10th September, when he would be glad to place the "superior-minded Princess" safely under the care of Sir Henry Halford (in whose ability Adelaide ever afterwards placed less reliance than her spouse). But to their bitter dismay Adelaide miscarried at Calais. Sad events now followed rapidly. In January 1820 the Duke of Kent inexplicably departed from the world in South Devon, leaving his Duchess, now twice widowed, with her daughter Anne Feodorowna Augusta Charlotte Whilelmina and her son Charles Frederick William Ernest, both by the previous marriage, her Russian lapdog, her songbirds and, most precious of all, her eight-month-old daughter Alexandrina Victoria. Kent, who was almost without a hair to his head, was only in his early forties. He had suffered not a day's illness apart from colds, and little physical injury since he had fallen off a horse while he was wearing some overtight pantaloons. He had fully intended to outlive his brothers. Unfortunately, he caught a chill at Sidmouth, developed hiccups and expired after imploring his distracted wife, "Do not forget me." She never did, any more than Victoria could forget the Prince Consort. Edward as an army officer had treated his soldiers as roughly as William his sailors. He had also cast off his 'old French lady' as casually as William had cut the hawsers which bound him to that generous woman, Mrs. Jordan, who had given birth not only to her master's ten children but had produced three more by another lover and one by 'S. O. Else'. But the hairless Duke of Kent was not the worst of the nation's trials and many mourned him. He was kind to his stepchildren and doted on little Victoria. No one foresaw the prodigious growth of his dynasty, which was to supply most of the thrones of Europe with kings and queens, and England with the greatest of all. Adelaide flew to Kensington Palace to comfort the Duchess. They read prayers together and became "real friends and comforts to each other". Despite the friction which developed later between William and his sister-in-law her friendship with Adelaide abided through all the trials.

A merciful release followed. The living wraith of George III escaped at last from mortal clay. For a long time the King had assured his devoted and favourite son Frederick, Duke of York, that he was already dead. On set days he wore mourning "in memory of George III, for he was a good man". He served Holy Communion to himself. He arrogated supernatural powers and threatened his doctors with hellfire. Blind, half-forgotten, his poor blistered head filled with fancies, the Sovereign roamed his rooms in a flannel night-gown and ermine-trimmed nightcap, playing the flute or the harpsichord, giving interminable audience to Ministers long since dead or dismissed. He died while the undertakers were still preparing Edward's corpse for burial.

3

The Path to the Throne

THE Regent, king in fact, had become George IV in name; and York was heir presumptive and confident of the throne. When his brother was crowned at the Abbey with mediaeval splendour Frederick exclaimed: "By God! I'll have everything the same at my Coronation!" But there was far to go. More tribulations lay ahead. In August 1820 Frederick's wife, the eccentric Frederica of the forty odorous little dogs, yielded up her spirit at Weybridge and the grotto knew her no more. The Duchess of York left instructions for her interment in the local churchyard next to her friend Mrs. Bunbury, and not at Windsor, where one day 'The Soldier's Friend' would be laid to rest beside her unless she took evasive action. The Duke burst into tears. England was to have no Queen Frederica after all—and, as events turned out, no King Frederick I either.

Nor was Adelaide to produce an heir to the throne. In December of this tearful year William's third daughter, Elizabeth Fitz-Clarence, wed the sixteenth Earl of Erroll, an ancestor of that Duke of Fife who was to marry the Princess Royal of the Edwardian era. A few days after the ceremony Adelaide was taken ill in the night at St. James's Palace. Straw was strewn about the approach roads, all door knockers muffled with cloth, and the whole purlieus wrapped in a deathly silence while the Duchess of Clarence struggled for two lives, her own and the unborn child. The morning of 10th December 1820 dawned bleak and uncompromising. At half past five she delivered the daughter who might have become Queen Elizabeth II. The child arrived six weeks early in the presence of the Duke of York, the Lord Chancellor and Canning as well as the suffering husband, torn between fear and hope. The new King sent word that the child was to be named Elizabeth, a name he had resolutely refused to have conferred on the little Kent niece Victoria. The Roman Catholic Lady Jernyngham wrote to her daughter Lady Bedingfield, who was to become one of Adelaide's ladies and her close friend to the end of her life, that the child was to be "a future Queen Elizabeth—but, I trust, not as sanguinary" as the first. Adelaide recovered to suckle her baby, but the task outran her strength. She lay quite ill for a month, and Londoners did not see her again until she drove in Hyde Park at the end of January 1821. Visitors were discouraged, but the door was always open to the Duchess of Kent and William's sister Sophia.

Mild February gave way to bitter March. The baby caught a chill. Three doctors maintained an unbroken vigil at her cot, but all their expertise was in vain. Adelaide went to see the convulsed and dying child and collapsed in William's arms. Elizabeth died at one o'clock in the morning of Sunday 4th March 1821 at the age of four months. Her death was the great disaster of Adelaide's life. Frequently afterwards the Duchess visited German spas to fortify her health, but she never bore another child. Twelve months after Elizabeth's death, when the little marble statue and her baby clothes were all that remained to remind her parents of her, the Duke was again writing with scarcely repressed excitement from Bushey that "in all probability the Dutchess is six weeks gone with child"; she was "particularly rude and has enjoyed perfect health since she resided at this place". They had settled discreetly in the great park adjoining Hampton Court, having decided to accept the £6,000 a year which William had refused, together with arrears, and were living the simple life. But Adelaide's pregnancy proved false, and William gradually surrendered hope of becoming the father of the next Sovereign. The public, however, never gave up wishing Adelaide into motherhood. Rumours that she was 'expecting' pursued her even when she was Queen and drew from William the wry comment that it was all "damned stuff, damned stuff, damned stuff".

Misfortune on this Wagnerian scale might have changed a lesser woman into a recluse or a misanthrope, but Adelaide

accepted her fate with prayers and patient meekness. Compassion
for others, her most outstanding characteristic, deepened into
maternal regard for all small friends and relations, especially for
the babies of her sister-in-law and her sister Ida. She concentrated
her thwarted mother-love upon little Vicky and on Ida's invalid
daughter 'Loulou' and her brother Wilhelm. The orphaned
Princess Victoria regarded William as her father; when the Duke
entered wearing his Orders she would clap her "little paws" and
run to him crying "Papa! Papa!"

These heart-warming encounters, which made William blubber
a little, kindled quite a different emotion in the formidable bosom
of the Duchess of Kent, who saw in them some kind of 'nursery
plot' to separate her from her child; for as time went on Victoria
grew fonder of Adelaide than of her mother. Soon after Elizabeth's
death Adelaide was writing to her niece: "My dear Little Heart,
I hope you are well and don't forget Aunt Adelaide who loves
you so fondly. Loulou and Wilhelm desire their love to you, and
Uncle William also. God bless and preserve you is the constant
prayer of your most truly affectionate Aunt, Adelaide."

Victoria was a healthy and happy child, but Princess Louise of
Saxe-Weimar had been paralysed by a spinal disease. For the rest
of her brief life she became the special care of Adelaide who
poured out her heart on her. William kept a cupboard full of dolls
specially for little girls. The collection was in charge of a servant
who, because of his features, was nicknamed Ugly Mugs, rather
tactlessly in a family some of whose members would scarcely have
won a contemporary beauty competition. When Victoria or any
other small girl visited the Clarences the Duke would say, "Now
my little dear, you can go and ask Ugly Mugs for a doll." Ugly
Mugs would pretend to fly into a passion when the request was
made to him in exactly the words the Duke had used. "My name
is *not* Ugly Mugs," he would say; and when they asked his pardon
he produced the doll. William with his quaint sense of humour
invariably burst into an asthmatical wheeze when the child, under
pressure, described the wrath of Ugly Mugs.

George IV began his reign with a major illness which left him
rather slimmer. On his recovery he almost collapsed under the
third heaviest blow of his life. The first had been the arrival of
Caroline for her marriage and the second the death of Princess

Charlotte. Now the unwanted Queen debouched from the Continent to claim her regal rights. Here was a feast for the readers of scandal sheets. Every piece of tittle-tattle about Caroline and her lover Bergami was magnified and coarsened in the narration. Few royal scandals before, and none since, generated more anguish at Court. Adelaide, caught in the current of events, was horrified by the intensity of public feeling against the King and members of the Royal Family. One skeleton after another grinned and clattered in the royal closet as the evil day approached when Lord Liverpool in July introduced the bill to deprive Caroline of the title and perquisites of queen consort.

When Adelaide saw to what depths the royal dignity could be degraded her fears for the established order revived, and she would never have been surprised to suffer the fate of Marie Antoinette. But the mood presently subsided and the *affaire*, although it must be reckoned among the precursive causes of the Reform agitation, was soon forgotten. Caroline's end was not far off when, with the benevolence which characterized the rhyming pamphleteers of the day, she was urged "to go away and sin no more; But, if that effort be too great, To go away, at any rate". Soon she was dead, still undivorced, still queen in name, more sinned against than sinning, at the age of 53. In her thirtieth year Adelaide, young enough to grieve for both parties to this monstrous charivari, felt compassion for her sister-in-law and read the accounts of her sexual eccentricities with rising dismay; but if she took any side in the dispute it was that of the King, who was invariably graceful to her. Had he not paid her the compliment of commanding her to name her infant daughter after England's greatest Queen? But the whole affair sickened her honest heart, and she was relieved when she was able to exchange England for the haunts of her childhood. At the end of June 1822 she and William sailed to the Continent in the Duke's yacht, the *Royal Sovereign*. The Duchess was an indifferent sailor, but she survived a raging night at sea with fewer marks of suffering than her maids and ladies, who were flung out of George III's great four-poster bed and rolled into the scuppers.

Once ashore William stretched his legs in hearty sight-seeing forays which exhausted his retinue. Cathedrals, museums, art galleries and Marlborough's battlefields engaged his unflagging interest. Then came duty visits to the relations: to Adelaide's brother of Saxe-Meiningen, who had spent so much time in England since her marriage that he was 'almost English'; and to the Queen of Württemberg, who had lived so long in Germany that her English was hard to understand. Charlotte was rapidly becoming grotesque. Her inflated torso was crammed into a voluminous evening dress, which she invariably wore in the daytime. Her face was already four times larger than when William had last seen her. As corsets to accommodate her immensity had not yet been invented, her stomach and hips were said to be "something quite extraordinary". On his way to see her William almost lost his life when his coach overturned at the foot of a crag near Stuttgart.

The Clarences, again travelling incognito but identifiably as the Earl and Countess of Munster, bowled along for three months, but they thought often of Princess Victoria. Adelaide was sad to leave her and sent her own and Uncle William's love to "dear little Xandrina Victoria" on her third birthday and begged her to give dear Mamma and "dear Sissi", her step-sister, a kiss in their name, also to "the big Doll". They were truly sorry not to be able to see their "*dear, dear* little Victoria" and hoped that she would not forget them. They were so happy to get home again, and their niece was overjoyed to see them again. But it was from this time that the Duchess of Kent began to keep William at arm's length, largely to cordon off her daughter from the noxious FitzClarences: it was not healthy for an impressionable child to be asking why Uncle William was their father while Aunt Adelaide was not their Mamma.

During the next three years Adelaide spared herself no pains to adjust herself to English ways, to adopt English manners and customs, and to insist upon the use of English materials in all her furnishings and clothes. She never did quite succeed. They were years of semi-seclusion, spent usually at Clarence House, which had now risen from the stableyard of St. James's Palace; sometimes at Bushey; occasionally on visits to George IV at Brighton, where the wife of the British ambassador to Paris could hardly take her eyes off her. Lady Granville thought her "a very excellent, amiable, well-bred little woman, who comes in and out of the room *à ravir*, with nine new gowns (the most loyal among us not having been able to muster above six), moving *à la* Lieven, independent of her body". The Lievens and the Granvilles who sipped the diplomatic honey at the Court of St. James's knew how to mix in the gall, but, then, time hung heavily on their hands and they had little better to do.

A conviction that the Duke and Duchess of Clarence must again visit the German relations crystallized in March 1825. Largely at Adelaide's instigation, they took George FitzClarence (the dear Queen of Württemberg felt quite unhappy at his not being legitimate) and his two youngest sisters, Augusta and Amelia—"not only very handsome girls but very pleasing, sensible and modest", thought their royal Aunt Charlotte. Before they reached Calais, that port of ill fortune, Adelaide complained of pain in the side and a persistent cough troubled her. The Duchess's doctor hoped she would be refreshed by Ems water and a change of air, and in the short term he was right. But her health afterwards never quite equalled the demands of public duty. William wheezed with asthma, which he temporarily shook off by walking four hours a day at Ems, putting himself also through a complicated series of physical contortions designed to tone up the stomach muscles and reduce the weight. For good measure he substituted sherry for green tea and dispensed with vegetables. On this occasion they stayed away six months. They saw Adelaide's brother married. They paraded the eligible Fitz-Clarence girls before the royal bachelors of Germany, but to no effect, as they afterwards had to settle for British bridegrooms of lesser rank. On their voyage home from Flushing the royal party suffered a discouraging experience. The *Royal Comet*, a paddle boat, steamed ahead of the yacht with a tow-rope. Two hours from the Scheldt a hurricane overtook them, and on losing one of her dinghies the *Royal Comet* threw off the tow-line and the two vessels wallowed to port by separate routes. Ultimately the *Royal Sovereign* landed her exhausted passengers at Yarmouth, William having shown towards his "illustrious partner" the most "delicate and uniform attention" during the ordeal, as befitted an admiral.

Misadventures of this kind did not deter William and Adelaide from setting out in the following March on their fourth, and last, voyage abroad together. Again they were accompanied by the FitzClarences, George and the youngest sister Amelia, but Mary (Mrs. Fox) replaced Augusta. Again the destination was Ems, where the royals flushed the kidneys, walked and rested. But

William impatiently dashed the party off to Quatre Bras, Belle-Alliance and the field of Waterloo, where he pointed out the exact spot where Blücher and Wellington had clasped hands. There the great Duke had almost been caught napping by the French cavalry. By God! it wouldn't have happened to him! And again the Clarences travelled as the Munsters. William had worn his second title so threadbare that it had a second-hand look when he eventually bestowed it on George. The travellers reached Calais in time to see Blanchard land his famous balloon safely; flying from Dover, he had been in danger of perishing in the North Sea before he adjusted his bearings. Once again on the cross-Channel voyage the tow-lines were blown adrift. After another frightening passage, which drew tears of admiration from all those who were well enough to notice William's beautiful devotion to his Duchess, they landed with prayers of thanksgiving. It had been hard to get home. But harder times lay ahead.

The completion of Clarence House now became William's obsessive pastime. His two brothers, George and Frederick, concentrated respectively on Buckingham Palace and Lancaster House, the latter variously known as York House, Stafford House and the London Museum. But the spectacle of elderly gentlemen creating sumptuous dewllings out of public funds while so many people lived in squalor caused a democratic outcry, in the middle of which the Duke of York died unexpectedly of gout and dropsy in January 1827, leaving heavy debts and an unfinished palace for the taxpayer to marvel over. At his funeral William remarked unfeelingly but correctly to Sussex: "We shall be treated now, Brother Augustus, very differently from what we have been."

William was heir apparent. Parliament added £3,000 to his annual income and gave Adelaide an extra yearly grant of £6,000. Her worth was at last appreciated at Westminster. The Lords were told: "If benevolence, amiability and virtue could give her a claim to regard and consideration, most fully was she entitled to them [cheers]. Not only did she seem possessed of every grace that could adorn the mind in her own domestic circle, but whenever occasion called her from home, she attracted affection by her kindness, and admiration by her benevolence."

Queen Adelaide

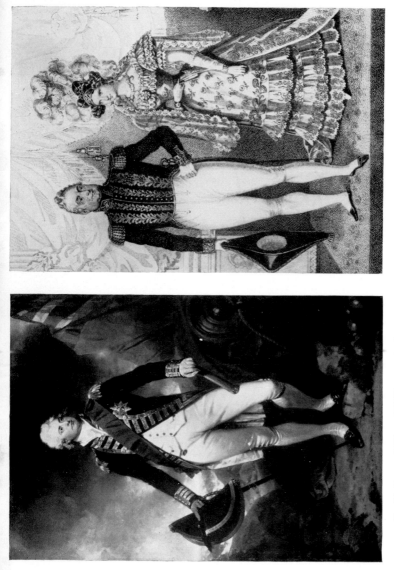

(*Left*) One of King William IV's favourite paintings, by M. A. Shee. He was Lord High Admiral of England at the time of the famous Channel 'adventure'. (*Right*) A sketch of William and Adelaide published in the closing years of their reign

A final compliment was the revival in 1827 of the ancient office of Lord High Admiral for William. The honour went to his head like an overdose of malt liquors. The Clarences moved into Admiralty House, where the Duke immediately regained his sea legs. Adelaide's decorous entertaining was swamped in a tidal wave of naval receptions during which the raucous-voiced captains of the King's Navy stampeded her drawing-room and scared the equerries and the ladies. Higher-bred guests, such as the wife of the Prussian ambassador, were caught up in shoals of red-faced jolly mariners and swept in and out of the reception rooms without ever once catching a glimpse of their hostess, who was submerged. The Duke himself escaped to a little room where the servants were washing up the china.

Adelaide was never more popular, for she was now certain to be queen. She spoke English still with a guttural accent and slipped into her native tongue whenever she could, for despite her best intentions anglicization still eluded her. Thus she was more natural than many of those who bobbed and becked around her in the hope of future favours. But her great trial was William. Power moved his freakish mind to strange acts. He bellowed orders from the bridge of the *Royal Sovereign*, quarrelled violently with that same Sir George Cockburn who had seen Napoleon ungratefully domiciled upon St. Helena, and tilted at John Wilson Croker, the Secretary of the Admiralty. On one celebrated occasion, seizing advantage of flawless summer weather at Plymouth in 1828, William signalled the Home Fleet to sea, leaving the distracted vice-admiral in command high and dry and choking with rage ashore. In his splendid uniform, ribbons fluttering and stars gleaming on the ample breast, the cockaded hat upon the pineapple pate, William paced the deck, breathed in the balmy sea breeze, issued streams of directions and gallons of rum, and disappeared down the Channel, where he and the fleet were mislaid for several days until he suddenly ordered the ships back to Plymouth. Even Nelson could have done no better. But William's quixotic behaviour brought retribution and he was dismissed. Adelaide was a long time forgiving Wellington for depriving her husband of the great joy of his life—to be Lord High Admiral in the tradition of Effingham. After all, he had only wanted to find out for himself what Nelson must have felt in the days before Trafalgar.

4

The excitement induced by the Channel escapade, by his brawls
with Cockburn and Croker about who was to be master at the
Admiralty, and his new eminence as George IV's inevitable
successor upset the balance of William's intricate mind, and there
is little doubt that he went slightly off his rocker in 1828. Princess
de Lieven, no unbiased Court clacker, discovered that the future
Sovereign had spent a whole fortnight in a straitwaistcoat.
Cumberland, his one sound eye frantically seeking out the main
constitutional chance, declared publicly that Brother William was
mad, like their father, and could not possibly reign.

Wiser people discerned that William was not so much mad as
revolted by the sanity he feared he detected in those around him.
Now the favour-seeking layabouts and ingrates began to court
him. Adelaide was visited at Bushey by no less than Lady Jersey,
who, it will be recalled, had played gooseberry at George IV's
nuptials with Queen Caroline. This was their first encounter; the
King's mistress had cold-shouldered her hitherto, and Adelaide
could but express surprise at a "pleasure so new and unexpected".
But Lady Jersey was one of many portents. The King was dying,
with a miniature of Mrs. Fitzherbert suspended on a black ribbon
from his neck. He was refusing to sign state papers. His dulled
eye focused heavily instead on the racing calender, for it was Ascot
time and essential to keep up an illusion of playing the horses.
For some time before his last illness he had been an object of
public indifference, with a body ballooned up like a feather-bed,
the grotesque outcome of years of compulsive eating and drinking.
Dropsy puffed out his legs like bolsters, and he used to visit
London like a thief in the night "when nobody could see his legs
or whether he could walk". He soused himself with laudanum
and brandy to ease the pain from his bladder, until drug and drink
alike failed to restore the colour to the leaden cheek or lustre to
the eye. Another sign of departing glory was the activity of the
two ruling spirits of his decline, Lady Conyngham—"the guard
wot looks arter the Sovereign"—and the former Plymouth
apothecary Sir William Knighton, who were making off from
Windsor with such royal loot as they had not already purloined
during their years of ascendancy over the King.

All that England required now was the word of authority. It
soon came. 'Poor Prinney is really dead', Creevey communicated
truthfully—for once—to his diary. The country took the shock

with composure. Few people mourned their monarch, but there were some who lamented him. "Dear, blessed King . . . dear Angel . . . adored brother . . . and in heaven will all his noble and generous deeds be registered, and who ever did more?" An interesting tribute from the kindest of George's sisters, Elizabeth. But there was a desiccated spinster whose estimation of the King was coloured by a relation, a Windsor canon. "Good riddance, say I," wrote Margaretta Brown. "I am glad we are going to have a *Queen*."

Adelaide presumably lacked Miss Brown's enthusiasm. She had not much enjoyed being the wife of the Lord High Admiral. Who could tell what might befall her on the uncharted seas of monarchy in a stormy age? Yet William had not gone mad, as Creevey predicted he must. He was King, determined to enjoy and relish, to cherish and enhance, the regal office. Adelaide for the moment thought it rather nice to be Queen, and William looked every inch a King. What others considered to be insanity in him was only high spirits after all. And what could be more pleasant when at first light on 26th June, a Saturday, Halford had galloped from Windsor to Bushey to announce George IV's death; and William, having hustled downstairs in his dressing-gown to have his hand kissed, hustled upstairs again and back into bed declaring that he was going to stay there for a while "as I have never yet made love to a Queen"? Then William's hero Wellington arrived. The Prime Minister was a little miffed to find that his late master's doctor had pre-empted him with news of constitutional importance, but he was also gratified that Adelaide no longer harboured any open resentment of his dismissal of the Lord High Admiral after the Channel spree.

The new king beamed from his coach all the way to London for the Accession Council. As most of his subjects had as yet no reason to suspect the cause they assumed the royal bows and handwaves to be yet another eccentric expression of the Duke's affability. At St. James's the King found it hard to remember not to shake hands with the Council members, who were his inferiors, begging each Privy Counsellor in turn to refresh his memory by a mention of his name as he toddled around the chamber peering kindly into each face like 'a respectable old admiral'. Baptized William Henry, he wished to reign as Henry IX, but the prelates in Council with a shudder reminded him of the ancient jingle:

"Henry VIII pulled down monks and cells, Henry IX would pull down bishops and bells." So on this exceptional summer day of 1830 he settled for William IV and, when he sat down to sign the proclamation, mildly complained, "This is a damned bad pen you've given me."

Penmanship was to try him sorely in the weeks ahead. Arrears of state documents required nearly 50,000 of his signatures. This deficiency William settled down patiently to supply, until his gouty knuckles cracked and swelled. However, he valiantly discharged his duty in daily doses, and striding forth on one of his 'constitutionals' through the castle gates, proudly displayed a red and puffy hand for the admiration of the sentries. Adelaide was the soul of solicitude during these 'writing' sessions and bathed and poulticed the swollen, ink-stained fingers. Even as Lord High Admiral he had never signed so many orders and decrees, such as one which dealt with a 'confidential naval matter', dated 13th December 1826, destined to be knocked down at a New York auction nearly a century and a half later for a paltry £5. (An autograph of Mr. Somerset Maugham, a widely-read twentieth-century novelist, was auctioned for the same price at the same time.)

One of those who welcomed the hasty departure of George IV's rapacious mistress, Lady Conyngham, but had no particular regard for Queen Adelaide, was the clerk Greville, who found the Queen "frightful, very ugly with a horrid complexion". Contemporary portraits do not fully bear out this sour description. A woman who saw Adelaide for the first time found her "insignificant" and "exceedingly plain", dressed in bombazine, with a little shabby muslin collar, dyed Leghorn hat and leather shoes. But this little "insignificant" Queen of 37 exerted over her excitable spouse an influence which no other women in his sixty-four years had ever equalled, not even Mrs. Jordan. In a dozen years of married life she had discovered how to bring him to his senses, partly by kindness, partly by showing him how any excessive impropriety in public damaged her reputation more than his. Certainly she did not achieve this influence by nagging or by any conscious effort to control him. The King was the King: he could be led, but he must not be lectured.

For the rest she jealously guarded his health, encouraging him to continue his walks, to breathe in the highly oxygenized air of

Bushey on rainy days, and by a good deal of huffing and puffing and gargling of beneficial saline waters, to prolong the monarchical existence. The people, after their disillusionment with George III and his eldest son, were ready to accept William and Adelaide at their own valuation. They wanted a queen and they wanted her with child, if possible. A Presbyterian minister prayed in this sense: "O Lord, save Thy servant, our Sovereign Lady the Queen. Grant that as she grows an old woman she may become a new man. Strengthen her with Thy blessing that she may live a virgin before Thee, bringing forth sons and daughters to the glory of God, and vouchsafe her Thy blessing that she may go forth before her people like a he-goat on the mountain."

Nothing could have been more considerate than Adelaide's and the King's treatment of Mrs. Fitzherbert. The reign was barely three months old when Maria was being received at the Pavilion with all honour due to the late king's married wife and regarded by the Royal Family as 'one of themselves'. At Windsor the King 'showed the Crown' to the people, flinging open the terraces for all to see their white-haired, red-nosed monarch sitting down to his mutton chop and sherry and then going off to his office to work. Great feasts were organized at the castle as William, with little thought for the strain imposed upon Adelaide, flung himself into the serious business of hospitality. But he did more to please than to upset his queen. The castle reeked of gas. The smell made Adelaide ill. William immediately had the supply cut off and oil lamps and candlelight restored. He was as careful of the Queen's health as of his own, and would wish his guests an early good night with, "I will not delay you from your amusements, but shall go to my own, which is bed with the Queen." But Adelaide worried when the royal euphoria beguiled the King into taking unescorted strolls outside St. James's, where he shook hands right and left, was thumped on the back, kissed by prostitutes and called "dear old boy" by pickpurses and other villains. He dearly loved being king. At his brother George's funeral, instead of walking solemnly after the coffin, he had nodded here, there and everywhere and clattered about among the pews pumping the hands of friends. He also caused gossip by giving the King of Württemberg a lift to Grillon's. Monarchs were supposed to accompany their peers only between castles and palaces, not to common taverns.

Courtiers expected Adelaide to act as a meddlesome fidget who would mould William to her will. In fact she reformed and re-organized life at Court with little fuss. Meals were usually served on time, the King's walks replanned to ensure privacy, sentinels posted at Windsor to discourage the crowds, and whenever possible the Queen attended receptions, interviews and reviews to protect William from those familiarities which might otherwise over-excite him. Nothing untoward happened when she was present. Adelaide also restored the image of 'the virtuous family' in public estimation, an image smeared by Lady Conyngham and other women who flaunted their favours at the Court of George IV. She was the true founder of 'Victorianism', for little Vicky learned from her Aunt Adelaide what she had not entirely learned from her mother, that what decent men expect from women in the last resort are modesty and decorum, at any rate in public. Adelaide deplored the loose *décolletage* of the Court ladies and successfully encouraged them to expose less of their bosoms.

The FitzClarences bickered, and Lord Erroll was extremely wroth with the Queen when she asked that his accounts as a Court official should be submitted to audit. Wishing to placate him for William's sake, she put a sweetmeat on his plate at dinner. He oafishly picked it up and tossed it back on to hers. But the public wanted to forget the trying progeny of Mrs. Jordan. The Queen calmed her ageing husband by making her peace with his children and keeping him home as often as she could, knitting by the fireside while the King catnapped in his chair, waking from time to time to remark, "Exactly so, Ma'am" in agreement with something she had been saying but which he had not heard.

"What a fortunate country this is to have such a Queen!" enthused Gabriele von Bulow. "May she be happy in her exalted position! She will be a saving angel for all the family."

Soon it was time to think about the Coronation. Had it been left to William and Adelaide the Coronation would have been dispensed with altogether for economy reasons. Rising demands for parliamentary reform and social justice threatened the Establishment. Adelaide appreciated the mood of the country more acutely than William. When Grey, who had succeeded Wellington as Prime Minister, reminded the King that he really could not reign without anointment and crowning William picked up the Crown, put it on his head and announced: "Now, my Lord, the Coronation is over." But it would not do. William had to be firmly led to Westminster Abbey. He thought not a penny more than £30,000 should be disbursed on the ceremony. The Government set a maximum target of £50,000. The actual cost proved to be £43,000, little more than one-tenth of George IV's Coronation expenses. Adelaide paid for her crown jewels out of her own budget and she dressed for the ceremony in a manner calculated to help English industry, especially the distressed Honiton lace workers: she ordered a robe of Honiton sprigs with a wreath of elaborately designed flowers—amaranth, daphne, eglantine, lilac, auricula, ivy, dahlia and again eglantine, the initial letters forming her name.

Undignified squabbles about precedence showed the Fitz-Clarences at their worst. The Duchess of Kent opposed everything, refusing to attend the Coronation, or to let Princess Victoria attend, if she was to be grouped as a dowager princess and peeress while her daughter was to take precedence after her 'wicked' uncles. The Duchess made an unusual and constitutionally improper demand to be treated as Dowager Princess of Wales and her daughter as heir apparent instead of heir presumptive. The 'Swiss governess', as George IV had called her, made things unpleasant for Adelaide, who deplored the worsening of relations between the Duchess and William and the fact that the Duchess now avoided her, too. There was an added reason for this coolness: Adelaide supported the claims of the Prince of Orange to the new throne of the Belgians against those of the ultimately successful candidate, the Duchess's bereaved brother Leopold.

The 'Half-crown-ation' took place on 8th September 1831 amid the domestic din and clangour and the rising public clamour for Reform. William submitted to the ceremony with heroic complacency and even agreed to be kissed by the bishops, an act of solemn osculation which he had earlier refused pointblank to tolerate: it was not seemly for elderly men to be kissing in public. Adelaide's dignified bearing impressed the crowds. Her "heartfelt devotion raised her above all outward surroundings". Madame von Bulow thought that although the Queen was "not too good looking" she appeared beautiful on this occasion. "It was the beauty of her soul that seemed to shine out from . . . her whole person." Parliament responded loyally by passing the Queen's

Dower Act, which nominated her Regent should a child of hers
survive the King. The Act also provided for her widowhood with
a settlement of £100,000 a year, plus the occupation of Marlborough House and Bushey Park.

4

Terrors of Reform

LIFE at Court in the early months of the reign flowed placidly enough. The King and Queen opened London Bridge, voyaging down-river from Somerset House in a fleet of thirty barges. We also get glimpses of drawing rooms, which Adelaide found so tiring that she usually bandaged her knee to reduce the fatigue of continual bending. Queen Charlotte would never have received an adultress at such functions, but when Lady Ferres insisted on attending, Adelaide, in order to spare her feelings, merely engaged in conversation with Princess Augusta and thus 'failed' to notice her. It was typical of the Queen that she could not bear to snub anyone.

The Sovereign and his Consort never forgot old friends such as the Clitherows of Bushey, who were invited to Windsor and St. James's Palace. But at Windsor they were usually surrounded by William's children and grandchildren. Sir Philip Sidney, his FitzClarence wife and their three offspring lived perpetually at the castle, although the husband travelled fitfully between Windsor and Penshurst to supervise the erection of his famous 'Place'; Miss Clitherow suspected it would be time enough for them to settle in Sussex should anything happen to prevent their "living on Papa". The King had given Augusta FitzClarence a house at Isleworth, but she preferred the home comforts of Windsor. And Lady Falkland, the last married daughter, frequently left her child with the King and Queen. The morganatic grandchildren frollicked in the corridors of the private apartments, calling Adelaide 'dear Queenie' and demanding dolls from the King. Young Prince George of Cambridge, lodging luxuriously

at Windsor while his parents slummed in Hanover, endured the
good-natured chaff of the Queen about his matrimonial intentions,
but it was hard to dispossess him until he suddenly branched out
on his own with an actress and morganatically produced his own
line of little Fitzes.

The castle often bulged with relations, such as the kindly
Duchess of Gloucester and her almost imbecile husband—the
other 'Silly Billy'—and her sweet but unwieldy sister, the Mar-
gravine of Homburg, so prodigiously stout (like the Queen of
Württemberg) that she could scarcely waddle. Adelaide, although frustrated child-bearing had affected her health, moved
gently among her guests with exquisite grace and cheerfulness in
her English silks, which she never tired of contrasting favourably
with French products. She was a passionate equestrienne, and
on her best days thought nothing of three hours in the saddle.
Dinner was usually served at seven o'clock, but if Adelaide had
not returned from her ride the guests had to wait. This appears
to have been the only flaw in a household otherwise remarkable
for its punctuality. On family occasions gold plate would be laid
for thirty or forty people in candlelight. After dinner the company
would divide up into tables, some to play cards, others to work at
embroidery or to write, while the Queen's musicians played
light music. Adelaide preferred knitting, sewing or drawing
to cards, and would invite members of the company to join
her while she showed them her sketches. William would scratch
through masses of state papers, ever signing, ever sighing, sometimes aided by his sister Augusta, who would hand him the
documents, blot them and put them in order. On Sundays the
Queen would take a book of sermons to St. George's and covertly
read it while the Dean droned for up to two hours, according to
the strength of the Divine afflatus. Adelaide knew all the Windsor
Park cottagers by name, and on her approach their children would
run out to the carriage for her to pat their heads and say just the
right thing. Whenever she watched children at play she wistfully
recalled her own lost Elizabeth, and would often weep afresh
over the white statue resting among the family pictures and
souvenirs of Altenstein in a castle turret room.

It was an ordeal for Adelaide to leave Windsor for Brighton.
Inexplicably 'Doctor Brighton' never suited her.

"I had to leave so much behind me," she wrote to Madame von

Bulow, "the beautiful country, my light cheerful rooms full of the busts and pictures I especially value, and above all the graves so sacred to me. To be near them does me good."

The Court moved to Brighton soon after the Coronation. With Adelaide went her sister Ida and her crippled niece Louise and the devoted Catholic lady-in-waiting, Lady Bedingfield. The Queen, hoping that sea bathing might benefit her 14-year-old niece, took her to the bathing establishment herself. But the mob made things unpleasant, and the child afterwards bathed in the sea. Soon after Louise arrived in London she had contracted chicken-pox. Neither Sophia, Sidney's wife and William's favourite daughter, nor the wife of Sir Herbert Taylor, the King's private secretary, went near her for fear of infection. Lady Bedingfield noticed with some asperity that they overcame their alarm when she recovered and the Court moved to Brighton and they could be 'seen' by more important people than by a crippled child with spots.

Almost since the accession the Reform agitation had been howling and yelping at Adelaide's heels. Uprisings abroad in 1830 ignited the British discontents which had been fuming and smoking since before her marriage to William. Now Greece had declared independence, the Belgians had seceded from Holland, and since a month after the accession the *bourgeois* King Louis Philippe had reigned in Paris while Charles X and his daughter-in-law, the Duchesse d'Angoulême, were exiled at Holyroodhouse Palace in Scotland. The plight of the Bourbons revived Adelaide's fears of civil war, for the new French revolution had prised the two opposing camps in England further apart. Philippe Egalité's triumph inspired the Reformers but stiffened the conservatives. Wellington and the Lord Mayor of London between them had stopped William and Adelaide from presiding at a Guildhall banquet, for their safety could not be guaranteed. Unfortunately, the Lord Mayor's name was Key. To this the Spanish title of Don was prefixed, so that he appeared in contemporary cartoons as the animal whose name he was supposed to bear. The King and Queen had been safe enough in the streets, partly because William was thought to have checked Wellington's reaction and to be sympathetic to Reform. But the King's failure to attend the banquet, although Adelaide was 'dying to go', encouraged the terrorists and almost led to a run on the banks. Cockney wits guffawed at William as "the cock wot's lost 'is courage". From that time Adelaide's popularity sank into sad decline; she was blamed for the rooster's conduct.

When Wellington fell from power the Queen was busy netting a purse after dinner at St. James's Palace. A note was brought to the King, who walked out of, and back into, the room without any sign to confirm rumours that he would abdicate rather than endure a Whig government under Grey. The news must have struck Adelaide with stunning force, but she continued at her worktable without pause or comment. She seemed to have resigned herself completely to playing the role of Marie Antoinette in the inevitable English Revolution. The new Prime Minister was a very different man from the Iron Duke, who understood so well what the dear country needed and was damned well not going to give it to them. Charles, the second Earl Grey, had succeeded Charles James Fox in the Whig opposition during the half-century of Tory supremacy which had now abruptly ended. At 66 he was an aristocrat of dignified appearance and stately eloquence. Moreover, he was a man of unblemished character, a rarity in a leading statesman then. But Adelaide shrank at the sight of him.

Mild though the reforms presented at Westminster through 1831 and 1832 now seem, they constituted a massive advance after a century and a half of parliamentary stagnation. There had been no change either in the franchise or in the distribution of seats in England and Wales since the Glorious Revolution of 1688. Consequently the expanding cities—Manchester, Birmingham, Leeds and Sheffield—were unrepresented in the Commons, while a ruined mound, a couple of niches in a mouldering wall, or a park without a house each sent two Members to Westminster. Private interests elected two-thirds of the chamber. A seat was valued at £7,000. Eighty-seven peers between them either nominated or used their influence to elect 218 of the English Members; another 137 Members were elected by powerful Commoners and sixteen by the Government itself.

Reform cleft the country from top to bottom, beginning with the Royal Family. At one extreme was Reform's arch-adversary, Cumberland, counterpoised by the liberal-minded Sussex at the other. When William refused to create enough peers to thrust

Reform through the Lords, it was Sussex who petitioned him from Bristol, urging him to cram on all sail. In the middle of the stage the King pirouetted between Whigs and Tories, a "half-comic, half-pathetic figure", it was said, vainly trying to rise above the seething party strife as the synthesis of patriot king. But it was upon his queen that the wrath of the Reformers fell.

Her Chamberlain, Lord Howe, was believed to exert a pernicious influence over Adelaide. As he was a fierce, uncompromising opponent of Reform, and voted against it persistently in the Lords, there was a popular belief that he was acting on Adelaide's orders. This was far from truth. Adelaide feared Reform because she thought it would mean the end of monarchy and the triumph of democracy. Howe would have resisted the Reformers whether he held Court office or not. In practice, of course, it is wise for peers either to abstain from controversy in the Lords if they hold Court posts, or not to serve the Court at all if they embrace politics; such considerations carried no weight then.

Princess Augusta saw in Adelaide a reflection of her mother Queen Charlotte—"never interferes or even gives an opinion. We *may* think, we *must* think, we *do* think, but we need not speak". This was not quite true, either. Adelaide did speak, and it was her cardinal mistake to keep at her side a peer as provocative as Howe. Where she might wisely have held her tongue, she spoke of the crisis to friends with a "gentleness and moderation" which really increased her involvement. Sir Herbert Taylor assured Grey that the King never "touched upon" politics with the Queen. "Even common articles of intelligence are not noticed, otherwise than as conveyed in the newspapers." Grey, unconvinced, deplored "the known opinion of persons composing Her Majesty's Household", as well as the declared bellicosity of the King's sisters—'the Sisterhood'. All this, thought Grey, could but foster suspicions that William was antagonistic to Reform. The King was traduced as the worst judge of men and situations to wear the Crown since James II.

Adelaide's unpopularity increased, and the mobs turned on her in the streets. On her return from a concert she was assailed by screaming demonstrators, who tried to snatch her out of her coach. The footmen lashed at the crowd with their canes while the driver whipped up the horses until the pursuers were left behind. The incident distressed the Queen. It threw William into a rage, and at the last minute he cancelled a pre-arranged official visit to the City the same night. Everywhere in the ranks of the Reformers the Queen was held up to ridicule as a narrow-minded reactionary who had come to England with her despotic notions from Germany and was trying to ruin a good king who knew what was right for his people but was forbidden to have his way. It was attractive pabulum for the propagandists, but it was almost grotesquely false. Adelaide's loyalty to Howe, her refusal to allow an untried and distrusted new Ministry to manipulate her household arrangements, were more to blame for her predicament than the Right-wing views she was supposed to hold. Mischievous lampoons represented Adelaide and her Chamberlain as lovers. One caricature shows Howe kissing the Queen, who is leading the King on a leash. Says the Queen, "Come along, Silly Billy"; and the King, made to look foolish and downcast, totters after her groaning, "Oh, I am a Poor, Weak, Old Man, they know I am not able to do anything."

Half the time the parties suspected of backstairs machinations were more intrigued against than intriguing. The King had apparently agreed with Grey to dismiss Howe after the Chamberlain had voted against the Reform Bill and the Lords had thrown it out, but William had neglected to inform the Queen. Her displeasure was visited upon Grey, whom she never really forgave, preferring to believe that the Prime Minister had forced the King helplessly into agreement. The Queen herself was writing to Wellington through Howe without telling the King. And without Adelaide's knowledge Howe was showing Wellington letters she had written to her Chamberlain. The Duke threw up his hands bemoaning that if public affairs went on like this the country would be 'lost'. "I can do no more in Parliament, I can do nothing out of Parliament." Howe felt his heart would break at the ruin he saw the Whigs—"such a set of imbeciles"—bringing upon the nation. Lord Eldon sank into even deeper melancholy. "My time is short," he told Wellington. "I am grateful to God that such is the case; being very confident that, if the bill passes, the Monarchy, and the Peers of the Realm, will not, as such, survive me long."

"The Queen is made ill by the worry which Ministers are

giving her," wrote Princess Lieven, "and the King's inside is rather upset by the same annoyances."

Adelaide saw Reform as an attack on the Church as well as on the state, and urged the bishops, not that they needed much encouragement, to unite to destroy the Bill in the Lords. That is what her detractors said. Whatever the facts, the agitators bodily assaulted some of the prelates and burned their effigies in the cathedral cities.

The Queen complained that she had been cruelly and unjustly insulted and calumniated, but she was not without champions. A pamphlet was widely circulated under the title "Appeal to the Honest Feelings of Englishmen on Behalf of the Queen of England". In the Commons a Radical, Sir Francis Burdett, frothed with indignation at the "insults heaped upon an illustrious lady, whose sex, and amiable conduct since her arrival in England, have given her claims to the respect and protection of all". Lord Winchilsea in the Upper House condemned the "infidel part of the public press" for its "envenomed slanders against an illustrious female holding the highest rank in Society, whose many virtues were the admiration of all classes in Society. Would to God that I knew who the vile slanderer was!" A remarkable letter which the Queen was said to have written to Brougham, the defender of Queen Caroline, appeared in the *Morning Post* and was later issued as a pamphlet. After denouncing the campaign against Adelaide as an attack on her private life, the latter continued: "The regal state is of itself sufficiently laborious and irksome, not to render those short moments of retirement too valuable and precious to be disturbed by Political Cabal."

The Times, which at first had defended the Queen, later when the Lords had proved intractable sneered: "A foreigner is not a very competent judge of English liberties, and politics are not the proper field for female enterprise." A retraction forced from the editor could hardly be described as generous. "Having without examination and under the excitement of such extraordinary intelligence published a statement which seemed to bear hardly on Her Majesty, we have sincere pleasure in giving it this contradiction, and in declaring our belief that the Queen is not capable of any underhand intermeddling with public affairs or of attempting what we are sure she could not accomplish."

The Sun ungraciously observed: "She, of course, is innocent of all intermeddling; and if she were not, how could her conduct be impugned? The King can do no wrong, the King and Queen are man and wife, man and wife are one flesh; ergo, the Queen must always be in the right."

While her adversaries spat every offensive epithet at the Queen, and the *Morning Post* called her "a nasty German frow", Croker wrote to a friend: "The King and Queen, and the Royal Family, are libelled, caricatured, lampooned, and balladed by itinerant singers hired for the purpose, to a degree not credible. They are constantly compared to Charles and Henrietta, and to Louis and Antoinette, and menaced with their fate."

A mob orator asserted that by her marriage Adelaide had been raised from "a state not so respectable or affluent as the lady of an English squire, to be the consort of the King of the most enlightened people on earth", among whom he clearly enlisted himself. "Pity the poor old King," read banners at an Edinburgh meeting. And Daniel O'Connell vituperously reminded householders of Westminster that Charles I had lost his head through listening to the advice of a foreign wife.

Reform Bill succeeded Reform Bill, to be passed by the Commons and thrown out by the Lords, and the country rocked on the brink of revolution. Prisoners in Derby jail were freed by force, a mob fired Nottingham Castle, tumultuous meetings threatened riot, 'Nosey' Wellington was hissed and stones were hurled through the windows of Apsley House. Cumberland was dragged from his horse while he was riding with Queen Adelaide in the park. In Bristol the 14th Dragoons refused to fire on ragtail revolutionaries even after the Riot Act had been read three times, the mutinous troops were ordered back to barracks and the city then half destroyed by anarchists. This last incident seems to have been the turning-point. It was at last obvious that the alternative to Reform was civil war. Yet William, when the Lords turned out the third modified Bill, still refused to elevate sufficient peers to force the measure through. The King said to the Earl of Munster: "Why, you know very well, George, as well as I do, that I never will make peers."

William's natural children shared the unpopularity of the Crown and the Queen during the agitation. "The by-blows of a king ought not to be his bodyguard," pontificated the *Morning*

(*Left*) Charlotte, Queen of George III, the austere mother-in-law to whom Adelaide was devoted. A painting from the studio of A. Ramsey. (*Right*) George IV, for all his faults, never failed in kindness and consideration to his sister-in-law Adelaide

The Sea King's daughter from over the sea. Princess Alexandra of Denmark with the Prince of Wales, afterwards King Edward VII, on their wedding day

Chronicle's armchair leader-writer. "Can anything be more indecent than the entry of a sovereign into his capital, with one bastard riding before him, and another by the side of his carriage? The impudence and rapacity of the FitzJordans is unexampled even in the annals of Versailles and Madrid." The unreliable Greville wrote that "all the Royal Family, bastards and all, have been perpetually at the King", who had suffered more from them than from his Ministers, which it seems hard to believe.

The truth may be that the FitzClarences as a whole began their sorry games at this time of grave danger, which they imperfectly understood, by opposing Reform. Then, when the Reformers were seen to be winning, they changed sides and threw the blame on their stepmother. At no time did any of the more responsible, or less irresponsible, of the King's children rally around William and Adelaide at this crisis, which might have cost them their lives. They constantly thwarted their father and added to his trials when pressures on him were so intense as to threaten his reason. The loyal Miss Clitherow found their conduct "abominable" and the manner of their address to the Queen "unpardonable". As for Lord Erroll, he "went on so bad in a public coffee-house that a gentleman cried out Shame! Shame!" Yet Adelaide had shown her stepchildren nothing but kindness. Her return was black ingratitude.

"Poor soul! her cough continues to wear her sadly, and she is hardly stout enough to contend with all her annoyances, notwithstanding the support of a clear conscience."

False or true, any statement or rumour which denigrated Adelaide and the Court fed the flames. The citizens of Birmingham, later to be a centre of Chartist infection, refused to pay taxes. Various local authorities, headed by the Common Council of the City of London, petitioned the Commons to withhold supplies until the Bill was passed. The Queen, who disdained to ride in a closed carriage, was pelted with clods of soil as she drove through Brentford on her way to London. The thought of flight never seriously seems to have entered her head. A story peddled by enemies alleged that she had persuaded William to flee secretly to Hanover, but the plan was discovered and came to nothing. The risks of such a course must have been unarguable: revolutionary England and France would at once have been involved in war with the monarchies of Austria, Russia and

5

Prussia. And who would then have played Wellington—or Cromwell?

The Reform bill became law on 7th June 1832. "Good-night to the monarchy, and the Lords, and the Church," said Croker, echoing Eldon and Wellington. But the turmoil gradually subsided as the country began to wonder what it had got for all its trouble. In retrospect the King and Queen seem to have been tested in the crucible of controversy and found not lacking in courage or spirit. Whether Adelaide's usual tact deserted her is problematical. She certainly appeared to have a blind spot about Howe. What were the facts of that unhappy discrepancy in an otherwise blameless life? Members of the FitzClarence family, notably Erroll, a peer of long and eccentric vintage who had been cellared in bottle too long, blackened Adelaide's character. Nothing, according to them, could explain her extravagant championship of Howe except a love affair. But there had been courtiers before Adelaide's time, and there would be afterwards, whose dog-like devotion to the queen consort of the day sprang from chivalrous dedication to duty, and even the prejudiced Greville conceded that much to Lord Howe. It was contrived that reports of a guilty liaison between the Queen and her Chamberlain should reach the ears of Howe's wife, who was "vexed to death". Lady Howe's Amazonian height and her strong will stimulated her eccentricity. Adelaide liked her, but she found some of her little ways disturbing. Once, when she was driving alongside the Queen, with Howe opposite, she lifted up her large feet and placed them first on her husband's knees and then thrust them through the carriage window, apparently to cool them in the breeze.

"What do you mean by shaking your head?" she asked when he remonstrated.

Lady Howe had fine legs, and at a bazaar she clapped her foot on the table to show how well a shoe fitted her. But beneath her flamboyance ran a deep vein of religious austerity. Sundays were sacred to her, when she did nothing but pray and read the Bible alternately. When the King invited her to a reception on the Sabbath she declined.

"If the King had been so urgent with me I could not have refused," said Adelaide, to which the Chamberlain's wife replied, "Madam, His Majesty is *your* husband."

By 1835 Lady Howe was dead at the age of 36, leaving a family of ten of whom the youngest child was only five weeks old. Howe did not long remain unmarried. People around the Court were mystified by his adulation of the Queen when his own wife was so outstandingly attractive. Was he not moved by Adelaide's isolation, and her bright nature, which shone out from the deeps of melancholy into which heartless treatment by the FitzClarences and the public's ignorant criticism sometimes plunged her? If Howe acted like a paramour it was hardly the Queen's fault. William shared his wife's attachment to Howe and shed tears when he was dismissed. Adelaide no less than her husband was loyal to old friends and could not, or would not, see that Howe's retrograde attitude to Reform besmirched the neutrality of the Crown. Her stubbornness was never shown to greater disadvantage than in the tug-o'-war over Howe's future. Grey's determination to supplant Howe with a nobleman more in tune with his government's aspirations clashed with Adelaide's inflexible will. She seemed to surrender when in 1833 Lord Denbigh replaced Howe, but she immediately took Howe to the theatre to show him that he had "done nothing to displease her". Lady Jernyngham sighed that the Queen was really so good and virtuous that she had no suspicion that people might think she liked Howe "too well". In the event Howe remained her unofficial adviser and confidant to the end of her life.

Over the Howe affair Grey sacrificed the Queen's regard, but she never showed open resentment. Rather she blamed the influence of Lady Grey, and was always "as cold as ice" to her. At Windsor the Queen went out of her way to bore Lady Grey by netting a purse or tatting away silently, as though her presence were of no particular significance.

During the Reform crisis the Queen outwardly preserved a calm which had a catalystic effect on her husband's morbid bouts of excitability. William lurched about in odd postures of irrelevancy. The Queen herself was kindness personified to those about her; she thought nothing of pushing her own anxieties aside in order to visit and console the Duchesse d'Angoulême, whose shabby treatment by the British government aggravated the distresess of exile. The Duchesse, as the daughter of Louis XVI and Marie Antoinette, was not only Charles X's daughter-in-law but also his niece. She was in her early fifties. Another of Adelaide's favourites was the Duchesse de Dino, the 'niece' of Talleyrand. This perceptive woman was entranced by the "perfect simplicity, truth and straightforwardness" of Adelaide's mind.

"I have rarely seen anyone in whom the feeling of duty is more pure," she wrote, "or who seems in all she says or does, more consistent. She is gay, kindly, and though she lacks beauty, she is most graceful; the tone of her voice is unfortunately nasal, but there is so much sense and real goodness in what she says that one listens to her with pleasure."

The Duchesse could have wished Adelaide to be "more English" and less German, especially in the presence of English people. But if the Queen had not been reproached for her German outlook she would have been condemned for something worse, for those who dwell in palaces are usually the prisoners not of fact but of other people's fancies. What could poor Sovereigns do? They could do no wrong yet were never right, so the Duchesse appeared to think. "Responsible for everything, they are continually assailed by accusations, well or ill founded. The poor Queen has already felt the bitterness of unpopularity, and of calumny. She has shown valour, dignity, and I am convinced she has plenty of courage for meeting danger."

The understanding Duchesse might have added to the catalogue of Adelaide's meekly-borne woes the tragedy of Princess Louise, who never recovered from chicken-pox and fell into a decline which neither the ozone nor the brine of Brighton could arrest. Her condition worsened during 1832 at the height of the Reform agitation, when Adelaide was frantic with anxiety. The child died in August, three months after the Reform Act passed. Her spinster sister-in-law, Princess Augusta, gave Miss Clitherow an affecting description of the closing scene. The King paid more attention to the detail of all Adelaide's wishes at the time of his niece's illness than he did to the importunities of the 'cabal'. The Queen emerged from the torment "miserably thin". This was the time chosen by the Duchess of Kent to mortify William and Adelaide by denying them the consolations of Victoria. Historians have found it difficult to explain or excuse the Duchess's conduct. In the spring of 1833 her two nephews, princes of Würrtemberg, visited their aunt. They attended a young people's ball at St. James's Palace. Victoria, who was about the age of the deceased Louise, was as affectionate as ever towards her Aunt Adelaide, who sat beside her between dances. But the Duchess was offensive and obdurate, refused to present the two princes to the Queen, and took them away early on the pretext that they were "tired" (which they were not when they stayed up late at the opera soon afterwards). When William invited the young men to Windsor the Duchess trumped up excuses, anything to avoid their coming into contact with the FitzClarences; they visited the Zoological Gardens instead, as Adelaide later discovered from the newspapers.

Another trial of 1833 was a visit to Windsor of Queen Maria of Portugal. She was 14. She had ascended the throne in 1826 at the age of 7 on the death of her grandfather John VI because her father, Dom Pedro, had become Emperor of Brazil and was ineligible for the Portuguese crown as well. Donna Maria's uncle, Pedro's brother Miguel, deposed her. Pedro renounced the Brazilian throne to fight for his daughter's rights. He also asked Queen Adelaide to undertake the child's education, having invincible faith in the ways of England, his country's oldest ally. But the Queen replied that she did not think a Protestant, even so high in the Established Faith as herself, could educate a Catholic, a sensible opinion with which any Catholic would have agreed. Years before, when Adelaide had first seen Maria, she had been a pretty child. But Lady Bedingfield was appalled by the distortions which so little time had wrought. Maria was far too stout for her age; her fat cheeks squeezed out her mouth and gave her a rather porcine look. Nor was she too well behaved. After overcoming her shyness at Windsor she made fun of Court worthies, tugged and pulled at Princess Augusta, and altogether conducted herself like "A Princess from the Sandwich Islands".

All honour was done to the visitors—Maria was escorted by her stepmother, the pretty ex-Empress of Brazil—but they upset arrangements on their first night at the castle by failing to appear punctually for dinner. Adelaide for once was kept waiting. She then sent Denbigh to announce that she wished to conduct her guests downstairs herself. They begged another half an hour. Adelaide finally went in search of them with Augusta, six ladies and Denbigh in attendance. She lingered tactfully in the corridors, making the usual courteous comments which no doubt all Queens have made on similar occasions, about pictures and statues and

busts, until at last the royal ladies were ready. They were as
abashed as their hungry hosts: it appeared that their luggage
had been delayed. Young Prince George of Cambridge almost
fled the castle when Adelaide told him he was to marry Maria,
whom he regarded as a "bloated doll". The Queen, always eager
to say something pleasant, remarked that her features were
regular and her bone structure was sound, and she would no
doubt improve. George was not one of the great wits of the day,
but it slowly dawned upon him that his aunt was joking.

The visit sapped the Queen's strength, and she was glad to
see Maria and her stepmother depart after three days. They were
in tears, whether of relief or gladness no one knows. Adelaide was
already suffering from rheumatism, which affected her breathing.
Her doctor ordered her to bed, where she slept for fifteen hours
under sedation, waking up much relieved. But her health had
deteriorated through strain and worry, through grief over
Louise, and from the Brighton climate. She was ready for a
change of air and environment. In the summer of 1834 she was
persuaded to take a holiday in Germany with the relations.
William felt he must stay behind: England needed him. He laid
the plans clandestinely and did not surprise her with them until
all had been arranged. The Queen was delighted, grateful for
this sign of his commiseration, but she was also torn between
the joy of seeing her aged mother and leaving William for six
weeks, for he had again begun to exhibit alarming symptoms.
Odd fits of passion alternated with flights of fancy. These were
noted by the Duchesse de Dino at the same time as she praised
the Queen's soothing influence upon the King. Adelaide had
begun to realize that she loved William more, and was more
necessary to him, than she had ever thought possible when she
left Germany. Now she understood that her only country was
England. All this made her departure in July painful to her, but
she was gently urged to leave, for if William during her absence
changed his Ministry no one could accuse her of having forced
his hand.

On the Continent she travelled as the Countess of Lancaster,
the incognito which Victoria afterwards frequently adopted when
she was Queen. In Saxe-Meiningen salutes by regiments, the
boom of cannon, church bells pealing, pretty girls in national
costume sprinkling petals before her, garlands of flowers and

festoons of foliage, greeted her everywhere. Ducal receptions and civic addresses brought the flush of pleasure to the wan cheeks. Adelaide was clasped to the ample bosoms of the Teutonic nobility. Before she left her homeland in August she bestowed 200 ducats on Altenstein towards the expenses of a new girls' school. A halt was made at Hanover on the return journey, and there she expressed the hope—a vain one—that she would soon return "with my beloved King and revered Consort by my side".

Grey's Ministry was still in office, although the architect of Reform himself had retired in favour of Lord Melbourne, destined to be Queen Victoria's first Prime Minister. Three months later, in November, the Sovereign suddenly dismissed the Melbourne administration, using as a pretext the death of Lord Spencer. Melbourne, who had thought it "a damned bore" to be the Sovereign's chief adviser, unaccountably disclosed his government's fall only to Brougham. This peer, whose devotion to mulled claret had caused him to address the Lords on his knees before the Woolsack when imploring them to pass the Reform Bill, had unfortunately sacrificed power for place by becoming Lord Chancellor contrary to the advice of his mother. He now took umbrage and a hackney cab to Printing House Square. *The Times* obligingly printed a few paragraphs recording the change of government: this was the first intimation which most members of Melbourne's Cabinet received that their successors required their seals. They were not noticeably amused. The indefatigable newspaper advertised its 'scoop' by plastering the streets of London with posters claiming: "The Queen has done it All". According to Erroll, whose indignation knew no frontiers, the Queen was an enemy to the people and, worse than anything, was very ugly and spoke English with a strong German accent.

For such gross unfairness there are few parallels. The attack on the Queen was based apparently on something which the prolix Princess Lieven had quilled from St. Petersburg suggesting that when Adelaide returned from Germany she appeared "somewhat put out" to find the Whigs still at the helm. A stream of poison oozed from Holland House in Kensington, for it was from the rival Apsley House that William derived the inspiration to exchange Whigs for Tories. Unfortunately the King involved Adelaide in the decision, for her usher, a young man of 24 named

James Hudson, was rushed all the way to Rome, through flood and stream over mountainous roads to find Robert Peel and beg him to return at the head of a Tory government. For this service, which almost cost him his life, Hudson was gratified to receive a bonus of £70. But the Peel Administration endured for only six months. William, forced to recall Melbourne and the Whigs, wept to the Duchess of Gloucester that he felt his crown "tottering on his head". This was a very different William from the Sovereign who had posted to the Lords in a democratic hackney carriage to dissolve Parliament a few years earlier after Lord Londonderry had held up his whip, roared, gesticulated, and threatened to maim a Whig peer if the Reform Act was passed; and after Lord Lyndhurst's language had sent Brougham skipping up and down in such a passion that no speaker could be heard above the uproar. If her intimates are to be believed, Adelaide had no hand in this 'plot'. The change of government was forced upon the King by politicians who feared the last authoritarian kick of Hanoverianism from the 'donkeys' of the City and their royal patron William IV.

The death of William in 1837 and the other misfortunes of that lachrymose year enfeebled Adelaide, but it would be an exaggeration to describe her as an invalid. At 45 she was young to be a widow, by modern standards. She had no inclination to re-marry. Since the time of Catharine Parr (who wed four husbands, two of whom had previously married six times) the queen consort of England was not expected to take another husband.

While William lay on his deathbed, the busy quill of King Leopold was spluttering guidance to his niece Victoria about that golden day when at last William IV was no more and she would be queen regnant. What an overpowering burden of responsibility—to advise, to encourage, to warn—rested upon the shoulders of the King of the Belgians, who but for the death of Princess Charlotte would have been Prince Consort of England! He had not forgotten that had Adelaide had her way he would not even be adorning the desirable new throne at Brussels.

When William died in her arms at Windsor his wife's first thought was that every honour should be paid to his memory. The Archbishop of Canterbury and Lord Chamberlain Conyngham, before they set forth on their historic mission to Kensington Palace, were solemnly enjoined to give Vicky a full account of her angelic husband's passing and expressly to tell her that, contrary to any report which may have come to her ears, the King's mind had turned to religion in his last days and he had died quite happily, his last conscious act having been to pardon a condemned felon. And would her dearest niece permit her to remain at Windsor Castle until after the funeral?

The new queen, after the shock of being awakened at five o'clock in the morning by two elderly gentlemen to be informed of her changed estate, was not lacking in duty to her bereaved aunt. She saw Stockmar, who stayed to give her some advice across the breakfast table. Then she wrote to her Uncle Leopold, such a tower of strength at a time like that, and to her half-sister Feodora, and followed this up by confirming Melbourne in office. These necessary duties discharged, she composed a long and sympathetic letter to Adelaide, addressing it to "The Queen", as she did not wish to be the first to remind her of her new status as queen dowager. Adelaide should remain at Windsor as long as she pleased. Much consoled, Adelaide replied gratefully to "my dearest niece". She had been deeply affected by all the sad scenes she had witnessed lately—the death of her mother, of Sophia Sidney and now of her lamented consort. But it afforded her deep comfort to dwell upon "the recollection of the perfect resignation, piety, and patience with which the dear King bore his trials and sufferings, and the truly Christianlike manner" of his death.

"Excuse my not writing more at present," she concluded; "my heart is overwhelmed and my head aches very much."

She signed herself "Your Majesty's most affectionate Friend, Aunt and Subject". In later epistles she abandoned this style and at Victoria's request signed herself her "most affectionately devoted Aunt Adelaide". It was a nice mark of respect from one crowned head to another.

William had died on 20th June. Six days later Victoria and her mother visited Adelaide at Windsor, the Duchess of Kent being anxious to assure herself that her daughter's inheritance remained intact. They had not been invited to the castle during the King's last illness, partly out of respect for Victoria's tender feelings— she was deeply attached to her uncle, a "good old man, though very eccentric and singular"—and partly because the sight of the Duchess at his deathbed might have undone the good work lately achieved by his spiritual advisers. And, of course, the place overflowed with fretting FitzClarences. Victoria prepared her aunt for the wrench of leaving Windsor by begging her to take two or three saddle horses, which now belonged to her, and anything else she pleased. In addition to the horses Adelaide took with her a silver vessel from which she had fed William in the last days. For his sake, too, she removed for safe keeping an oil painting of William and all the FitzClarences *en famille*, which depicted Mrs. Jordan busy hanging a picture on the wall and showed also a bust of the King on a pedestal. "It was a picture better out of sight for his memory," Miss Clitherow decided. And with her went, of course, her most treasured possession, the marble effigy of little Elizabeth. Before she retired to Bushey, while Marlborough House was being made ready as her town residence, she wrote thanking Victoria for all her indulgence "since it has pleased our Heavenly Father to put you in possession" of the castle.

Adelaide's apotheosis from queen consort to queen dowager was no great trial for her. It is hardly credible that she had not enjoyed being queen, despite the unquiet and often tragic times through which she had passed. But she was not well, the sorrows of 1837 had further undermined her health, and she was glad to settle quietly at Bushey, where she had spent most of her married life. Half her income of £100,000 was now spent in helping others: she thus created the precedent for queen mothers of a lady bountiful supporting, as far as possible, the good work of the modern Crown. She subscribed heavily to charities in the parish of St. Martin, in which Marlborough House lay, to the Society for the Propagation of the Gospel, the Colonial Bishopric Fund and other eleemosynary causes. When Queen Charlotte had married George III provision was made for her to spend her widowhood in Mecklenburg if she wished. The Cabinet proposed a similar arrangement for Adelaide, but William, deciding rightly that his queen would never want to return to Germany, omitted to tell Adelaide of it.

By a cruel tradition dating back to the Plantagenets the Queen Dowager was not permitted to attend Victoria's Coronation, but on that glorious day she wrote to her niece: "The guns are

just announcing your approach to the Abbey, and as I am not
near you, and cannot take part in the sacred ceremony of your
Coronation, I must address you in writing to assure you that
my thoughts and my whole heart are with you, and my prayers
are offered up to Heaven for your happiness and the prosperity
and glory of your reign."

Adelaide's prayers were to be richly answered. In the same year
she began a series of travels abroad in search of sun and health.
From Malta, where she spent three months and founded the
Collegiate Church of St. Paul at Valletta, she wrote to the Queen,
who, beset by the rigours of an English winter, was moved
by her aunt's descriptions of orange trees and other tropical
plants to observe that they "do tantalize one a good deal, I do
own". Adelaide returned more cheerful and in better heart,
and soon she was writing to congratulate her niece on her
engagement to Prince Albert—"an event", the Queen assured
her aunt with all the sweet confidence of youth, "which so nearly
concerns the future happiness of my life".

Arrangements for her appearance at Victoria's wedding helped
Adelaide over the early phase of her widowhood. The death of
William and the Queen's accession had drawn her closer again
to the Duchess of Kent, and they 'exclaimed' over the same things.
No one rejoiced more than the Queen Dowager when on 21st
November 1840 Victoria gave birth to the future Princess Royal,
who became Adelaide's godchild, Victoria's closest confidante
and future Empress of Prussia. But Adelaide untactfully irritated
the Queen in the same year when the Whigs under Melbourne—
having allowed their reformist ardour to embroil them with
Jamaica over the freeing of slaves, and with fresh troubles loom-
ing in Ireland—resigned in favour of Peel and the reconstructed
Tory Party, now officially to be called Conservative for the first
time. Once again Adelaide's good sense deserted her, for she
wrote to compliment Victoria "on the good grace with which
she had changed her Government". Although the departure
of Melbourne must have been "very trying", she trusted the
Queen would have "perfect confidence in the able men who
form your Council. Our beloved late King's anxious wish to see
Wellington and Peel again at the head of the Administration is
now fulfilled. His blessing rests upon you." The Queen, whose
relations with Melbourne were almost those of daughter and

father, was not conspicuously felicitated by these expressions of her aunt's interest in the political situation. There was one other upset. Adelaide fancied the Queen had advised her to refuse to be godparent to the son of Prince Hohenloe-Waldenburg because the child would be reared as a Roman Catholic. In fact, Victoria forgot all about it and decided to sponsor the baby herself. Adelaide was considerably annoyed; but only one Queen can do no wrong at one and the same time.

Vainly searching for health, Adelaide moved about the country from one stately home to another. We find her at Belvoir, or at Witley Court, Lord Dudley's seat in Worcestershire; and for a while she rented Cassiobury, Lord Essex's house near Watford. Her last few years were sweetened by frequent visits from her sister Ida, and Ida's son Prince Edward of Saxe-Weimar lived almost entirely with Adelaide. Duchess Ida stayed with her sister at the Harcourts' at Nuneham, where Wellington was also a guest, and where the Archbishop of York fell while walking with the Duke.

"If I am hurt," said the Archbishop as Wellington helped him to his feet, "it is on a side on which your Grace never gave the enemy a chance of hurting you."

Usually Adelaide travelled by train for the longer journeys. She liked modern steam travel, whether by land or sea, although she left Cassiobury because her sleep was disturbed by the thunder of express trains and the language of bargees on the Grand Junction Canal. She was also distressed by some of the more sanguinary relics of Charles I's execution which found a depository there. Most of the FitzClarences remained on good terms with her, and William's grandchildren brightened her widowhood at Marlborough House, where Lady Munster particularly recollected the old Queen's wonderful pink and grey cockatoo. But her cough had become so troublesome that she could not face another winter in England, and in October 1847 she sailed for Madeira, which she had refused to visit earlier to avoid spending her income outside the Queen's dominions. A large party accompanied her, Ida and several children included. Adelaide's liberality knew no bounds: in addition to pouring largesse on the poor she built a new road for local fishermen at her own expense.

On her return in April 1848 she knew she would never travel abroad again. She was lonely and ill. After the death of Princess Sophia in May, only two of George III's huge family survived—the inelegant Cumberland and the half-demented Duchess of Gloucester. Her affections centred in Victoria's babies, to whom she gave handsome presents. Her warm heart also turned towards the exiled Louis Philippe and Queen Amélie, who after the upheaval of 1848 had taken refuge at Claremont.

"Nothing could be kinder," Victoria told Melbourne, "than the Queen Dowager's behaviour towards them all."

The need for peace and quiet moved Adelaide to rent Bentley Priory, the Marquess of Abercorn's house at Stanmore, and there she settled down to die. In November 1848 the Queen and the Prince Consort spent two days with her, and a year later they saw her at her Middlesex retreat for the last time. She then never left her room. Paroxysms of coughing, broken sleep and a fatalistic feeling that life was ebbing away exhausted her. Victoria wrote to her Uncle Leopold: "There was death written on the dear face. It was such a picture of misery, of complete *anéantissement*—and yet she talked of everything. I could hardly command my feelings . . . and when I kissed twice that poor, dear, thin hand —I love her so very dearly. She has ever been so maternal in her affection to me. She will find peace and a reward for her many sufferings."

Two days before she died the Duchess of Kent called, but by that time Adelaide had ruptured a blood vessel in the chest and was almost too weak to speak.

"Much was done to set Mamma against her," wrote Victoria, "but the dear Queen ever forgave this, ever showed love and affection, and for the last eight years their friendship was as great as ever."

Adelaide drew her last breath on 2nd December 1849 surrounded by relations and friends, including Ida and Edward.

"She is a great loss to us both," grieved Victoria, "and an irreparable one to hundreds and hundreds. She is universally regretted, and the feeling shown is very gratifying. . . . *All* parties, *all* classes, join in doing her justice."

Yes, when it was too late. Her burial instructions had been set down eight years earlier in her own clear style and hand:

I die in all humility, knowing well that we are all alike before the Throne of God, and request, therefore, that my mortal remains be conveyed to the grave without any pomp or state. I wish to be moved to St. George's Chapel, Windsor, where I request to have as private and quiet a funeral as possible. I particularly desire not to be laid out in state, and the funeral to take place by daylight, no procession, the coffin to be carried by sailors to the Chapel. All those of my relations and friends, to a limited number, who wish to attend, may do so [here she mentioned a few intimates]. I die in peace and wish to be carried to the tomb in peace and free from the vanities and pomps of this world. I request not to be dissected nor embalmed, and desire to give as little trouble as possible.

All proceeded according to her wish on a dull, foggy morning whose funereal atmosphere was relieved only by the red coats and burnished helmets of the troops who accompanied the coffin through Ruislip, Uxbridge and Slough. At Harrow the bells tolled and boys in weepers and black scarves walked with the mourning coaches for a short distance. Albert towered above the mourners, but the Queen was *enceinte* and remained indoors at Osborne. Two of the FitzClarences, Frederick and Adolphus, were pall bearers. Truly the follies as well as the vanities and pomps of this world were forgotten as Adelaide was lowered into the tomb next to William on 13th December after Howe and Denbigh had broken their staves of office over the casket. Shortly after her death her household goods were auctioned on the premises at Marlborough House, which was settled on the infant Edward, Prince of Wales, so that it could become his official residence when he should reach the age of 18.

More than 100 people were remembered in Adelaide's will. She had piously devoted much care to the document, so as to ensure that the beneficiaries received what would please them most. For instance, among other bequests her sister received the last piece of needlework completed by Princess Louise. A bust of this niece and one of William, both by Chantrey, were left to her brother. Her eldest nephew received a Bible which her mother had given her on her confirmation in 1805 and was her "greatest treasure and consolation". To the Duchess of Gloucester she left William's last present to his Queen, a diamond bracelet which Adelaide received the day before he died, and a portrait of the King which Princess Augusta had bequeathed to

Adelaide. Even the FitzClarences were remembered. Rings were left to the stepdaughters, and to the stepsons went all the pictures in the Bushey gallery and several memorials of their father. But a Bible and writing materials which she willed to Lord Howe were ignored by the authorities to avoid a revival of malicious gossip.

To Queen Victoria, her dearest surviving niece, went the dearest possession of all. The marble statue of the child who might have been queen, and whom she still mourned on her deathbed.

Queen Alexandra

5

At the Zenith

SCOULAR's marble effigy of Princess Elizabeth of Clarence lay undisturbed at Windsor during the sixty-four years of Victoria's reign. In the spring of 1901 a mellow voice with a light Nordic inflection echoed in the castle corridors.

"Whoever could that child have been?"

The new king, Edward VII, casually removed an inch of ash from the tip of his Havana cigar.

"If that child had lived, my dear," he drawled loudly enough for her to hear, "you and I would not have been here now."

Queen Alexandra was only five years old when Queen Adelaide died. She was unaware of Elizabeth's brief existence. While Victoria lived very few people ever saw the inside of her private apartments; Alexandra was not one of the few. The Princess of Wales stood so much in awe of her mother-in-law that it was only after her burial that she permitted anyone to kiss her hand or to address her as "Your Majesty". Critics of Edward's consort have attributed this quirk to waywardness, but Alexandra had lived nearly forty years in the shadow of her husband's mother. Now that she could "do as she liked", in her own phrase, she paused reverentially on the threshold of power. It took her a little time to play first lady on a stage for so long impregnated by the overpowering personality of Victoria.

The first task was to spring-clean the monarchy. Sovereigns have rarely engaged themselves in this Augean task with more exuberance than Edward and his Queen, who, at the age of 56, was yet the most beautiful woman of her day. Together they brought about remarkable changes, bewildering for the late queen's Hindu *wallahs*, who padded like lost dogs about the dust-laden spaces of castle and palace, dumbly following the removal men as their mistress's treasures disappeared to accommodate Alexandra's "beautiful things from Marlborough House". The King quailed before the upheaval. Like William IV before him, he would have been ready to hire Buckingham Palace to the army, even to Parliament, and flee to Hampton Court. As this was impracticable he flung himself into the iconoclastic process with much noise and motion, often in his shirtsleeves, looking like a foreman. Lord Esher, rising to eminence at Court, deplored the "too human" touch that might diminish the royal dignity. Yet one improvement even appealed to him. The King ferreted out of the old queen's rooms several memorials of John Brown, the Knox-like Highland ghillie on whom his mother had lavished such inexplicable favour. It gave him immense pleasure to trample the pictures and 'photos' of his old enemy underfoot and tumble the busts and statues on to the rubbish-heap.

Bickerings and badinage enlivened the ceaseless sessions of interior decorating at the royal residences. As Alexandra was now very deaf and the King had to shout in her ear, the art expert, Sir Lionel Cust, occasionally marvelled at the things he heard. One courtier felt the new occupants of Windsor were taking an unpardonable liberty; he found it strange to see "dear old Mr. Wayte", the aptly named page, toddling after the King, and stranger still to see some Indians hovering uncertainly behind the new Empress's chair. Animated receptions in the Green Drawing Room, glittering suppers in the White Room, replaced the sober entertainments of the old queen in the dingy Oak room. The King played whist until one in the morning while Alexandra —"full of rag and mischief", Esher noted—rocked the Green Room with mirth. Sometimes the Queen played patience or bridge, but in the early days refused to stake money on the game, objecting that she did not yet know whether her parliamentary allowance would run to it.

The new Sovereigns delayed their first public appearance until the state opening of Parliament on 15th February 1901. Then, as now, the dimmed lights in the Lords chamber flared into full radiance at the royal entry. There was a gasp and a flutter of astonishment as Alexandra was revealed, her hand on the King's, a serene, girlish figure, a study of transcendental loveliness in a deep-black gown set off by the brilliant scarlet of her state robe. A thick rope of pearls fell to below her knees. The Koh-i-Noor in her crown dazzled the beholder no more than the Queen who wore it. At first Alexandra looked slightly nervous, but she soon recovered. Esher thought she lost some of her tone (he was an expert on royal manners) when she smiled and nodded at aristocratic friends and paid a little too much attention to the faithful Commons jostling at the Bar behind Mr. Speaker Gully. Two days earlier the King by special statute had created her a Lady of the Garter; no woman had been admitted to this ancient Order of chivalry since the reign of Henry VII. Her marriage to Edward had often been subjected to agonizing strains. The King, possibly under the impulsion of a guilt complex, determined to uphold her prestige as queen in every possible way. Some luckless official who proposed that when the monarch was out of London the mounted guard at Whitehall should be reduced was told curtly: "The Queen will always have the same travelling escort as myself."

Whatever had divided them in the past, the new reign was to be a business, and certainly a businesslike, partnership. The Queen telegraphed to a countess: "The Queen would like your daughter to come into waiting for Windsor. Crêpe veil and high stuffed dress for dinner."

Ironically, while Alexandra chopped right and left through the mound of sentimental baubles piled up by Queen Victoria, she herself had become an intransigeant gatherer of *bric-à-brac*. She could never part with anything. Books, china, old faded letters and theatre programmes yellow at the edges, menus, bits and pieces of ribbon and lace, Earl's Court china pigs and bogwood tokens from Ireland, a fishing fly from Scotland or a maharajah's brooch from Behar—all these cluttered up the royal apartments as the Edwardian era surged into the new century. Musical nephews demurred when Alexandra asked them to play the piano, for it was so weighted down with trinkets and 'photos'—even the music stool—that they feared it would take an hour to put everything back.

At the coronation in 1902 the Queen made an even more sensational impact than at the state opening.

"I shall wear exactly what I like," she decided, "and so shall my ladies. . . . *Basta!*"

She also meant to be queen in fact as well as in name. The usual style of queen consort might imply that the grandeur and the glory of queenship had dissolved with Victoria's passing. But Alexandra had played second fiddle long enough to a queen regnant: she would refresh the faded glory and give the title of queen a new dimension. Courtiers marvelled at her obduracy. There had been no crowning for nearly two-thirds of a century, and this was the first 'Empire' Coronation. While officials, like terriers with buried bones, uncovered various precedents of doubtful validity, the Queen stamped her foot and made her own plans. She announced that she would be attended by four duchesses—tall, beautiful and all alike. The height of the fald-stool in the Abbey was decided by the Queen alone; after all, it was she who had to kneel on it.

When Edward fell ill he sent Alexandra to Ascot to disguise the truth; he would never agree to postpone the coronation.

"Afterwards," he told his doctors, "you may cut me in two, but I cannot—I will not—disappoint the people."

Sir Edward Treves, the Serjeant-Surgeon, replied dryly that if the King went to Westminster Abbey before surgery it would be in his coffin.

The King's operation for perityphlitis has passed into medical history, and at this length of time Alexandra's anxiety can be only surmised. Throughout the emergency, the second she had endured on account of her husband's health, she showed the world a brave face. On his recovery she personally supervised his departure for the Isle of Wight for the convalescence aboard the royal yacht *Victoria and Albert*. Sailors arrived at the palace with a chair to carry the King from his bedroom. The Queen commanded an equerry to sit in it, then paced out every step of the way through the tortuous corridors to a closed omnibus behind the palace. Next day this painstaking rehearsal ensured the King's passage to the island without accident. Aboard the yacht Alexandra's gaiety and light heart—some historians would say her 'silliness'—did more for Edward than his doctors and nurses. One day Kitchener was piped on deck. The King laid the Order of Merit around his neck. Alexandra burst into tears. The imperial hero, with his 'mudguard' moustache, inspired in her an almost mystical affection. Fourteen years later she had a premonition that he would never come back alive from wartime Russia. But duty called, HMS *Hampshire* went to the bottom of the sea, and history probably took a different course because a 'silly' woman's sixth sense was ignored. Another celebrity who fascinated the Queen on the yacht was the Bishop of Winchester; she persuaded him to smoke his first cigarette with her and laughed at his episcopal grimaces.

The coronation took place in August on a reduced scale. Alexandra was hailed as the most beautiful queen who had ever entered the Abbey. She had pondered much beforehand on the religious meaning of the ceremony, as distinct from its pageantry; consequently she infused into the crowning an ethereal quality to be compared with a Papal enthronement. Sir Almeric Fitzroy thought few witnesses would ever lose the recollection of four of the loveliest women in England, with their trailing purple robes and sumptuous apparel, supporting a canopy beneath which the stately figure of England's queen received the holy oil; and when the group dissolved it seemed like "the passing of a dream". A less celestial chord was sounded by Princess Marie Louise. The Queen was perturbed, she reported, because "a drop of the Holy Oil with which she had been anointed had trickled down on to her dear little nose, fear of irreverence preventing her, as she told me, from using her handkerchief!"

So Alexandra, as Mrs. Browning might have mused, with a sceptre as light as a fan, beating sweet time to the song of life, went her regal way. Sir Hall Caine, the Manx novelist, saw her in the Isle of Man. The King said scarcely more than a dozen words at a time, but the Queen "talked continuously, hardly ever waiting for a reply". He was apparently ignorant of her deafness. She was "all nerves and emotions", struggling to control both in order to spare, or not to displease, the King. The novelist impulsively suggested that the ceaseless thumping of the salute guns should be stopped. Alexandra disagreed—"The King would not like it."

The royal wills clashed, not for the first time, when on his birthday the King forbade Alexandra to attend the Trooping the Colour ceremony: she must sit quietly in a palace window and watch the final march-past with the Duke of Connaught, his brother. The Queen fell into an ominous silence, as she usually did when her wishes were opposed. Edward rode away, but as his back disappeared down The Mall she rose with an imperious: "I go!" Her carriage was ordered to catch up the procession, she

joined it almost unnoticed, and after the parade returned before
the King found out. She thought it "funny".

Around this time Sandringham, which Alexandra always regarded
as her home from home, was favoured with a visit from the
Emperor Wilhelm II, who was Edward's obnoxious nephew
through his eldest sister. From his youth the All Highest had
displayed a positive genius for ruffling his Uncle Edward. The
Kaiser reacted upon Edward and Alexandra like a wasp at a
garden party. He was always trying to 'boss' his uncle. He would
have stage-managed the coronation but for the tradition which
excluded the attendance of crowned heads. But Willy was incorrigible. A few months after Victoria's death his mother, the
Empress Frederick, followed her to the grave at the end of a life
unpleasantly marred by a tendency to order, domineer, interfere,
and offer tactless advice to her numerous relations. She had nevertheless contrived to bring about the marriage of her brother to
Alexandra; and, as she had been abominably treated by her son
after the short reign of the Emperor Frederick, many tears were
shed for her when at last she escaped from her troubles to the
Potsdam mausoleum. At the funeral Alexandra, who only by a
supreme exercise of self-control could ever be induced to visit
Berlin, was intensely annoyed by the display of military pomp.
Willy's bombast still rankled when he visited Sandringham in
1902 for the last time. The more Edward retreated into a hard
shell of avuncular reserve, the more savagely he bit into his cigar,
the more expansive Willy became. Only the Queen's tact enabled
the two monarchs to keep their tempers. Willy, having driven in
one of the King's motor-cars, told his uncle he was using the
wrong fuel. Potato spirit was the thing. He immediately telegraphed to Berlin, and an assortment of bottles and phials
descended upon Sandringham. Tranquillity was restored by an
effort which left Alexandra "perfectly exhausted", and when the
King to keep up appearances saw his nephew off at Portsmouth
he spattered cigar ash all over the quayside and exclaimed,
"Thank God!"

The hagiology of the Edwardians contains few favourable
references to Wilhelm. He was the layer of faggots and lighter of
pyres beneath the saintly jugglers who were striving to maintain
British imperialism, world peace and the balance of power in

Europe. By 1904, after the *Entente Cordiale*, the German Emperor
and his British relations drifted further apart and Alexandra,
ever sensitive to the fortunes of Denmark, pirouetted into a
political situation potent for future evil. In October the Russian
Baltic Fleet, cruising through the North Sea on its way to confer
upon the Japanese navy one of its greatest victories, shelled some
Hull trawlers off the Dogger Bank, incredibly confusing them
with Japanese gunboats. The "damned fools" of Russians, as
Edward called them, were slow to apologize and slower to compensate, and for a time the issue of war between the Russian and
British empires quivered in the balance. Alexandra, whose younger
sister Dagmar was the Dowager Empress of Russia and whose
son the Czar Nicholas uncannily resembled his cousin George,
Prince of Wales, delicately stepped upon the tightrope of personal
diplomacy where so many disparate elements were heatedly
maintaining a precarious equilibrium. Her intervention appears
to have relieved the tension, but it also had the effect of thoroughly
arousing Willy, who vowed that if a British fleet should dare to
storm the Baltic he, and if possible the Russians, would occupy
Denmark and close the Kattegat. The Kaiser's sister, who was
married to Crown Prince Constantine of the Hellenes and had no
particular reverence for her imperial brother, alerted the relations
in London to this anti-British plot. Meanwhile Willy had put the
case for a 'peaceful' occupation of Denmark to King Christian,
who at 86 had not far to go in this world. Christian's repugnance
for Germany, at whose hands the Danes had suffered much,
equalled his devotion to Alexandra; and when his favourite
daughter expressed "horror at the bare thought of *betraying*
England", the King concurred with her sentiments. The Kaiser
retired crestfallen from Fredensborg.

The Prussian Emperor had increased Alexandra's Germanophobia by lauding Frederick the Great as his idol and assuring his
aunt that his dream was to be like him. Nor could she forgive
Willy's ill-treatment of his mother. She once unburdened herself
to Paul Cambon on the subject of her nephew.

"He adores noise," she told the French ambassador; "he
meddles with everything, he *will* play the part of Charlemagne and
domineer over all the Sovereigns, he *will* undertake everything at
once, and though he always assumes an air of assurance and
superior knowledge, he is often mistaken."

The next clash with Wilhelm was a personal one. In 1905 Norway broke away from Sweden. Alexandra devoutly wished to see her youngest daughter Maud upon the new Norwegian throne as Consort of Prince Charles of Denmark. Another candidate was pressed by Willy, who by this time regarded Edward as the "arch mischief-maker of Europe". All her wiles and artifices were used to good purpose. Charles became King Haakon of Norway, and Alexandra rubbed in the humiliation by persuading Edward to invite the new Sovereigns to London before Berlin.

In June 1908 'Bertie and Alix', the British Sovereigns, organized a family reunion with 'Nicky and Alicky', the Russian Czar and Czarina, aboard the yachts *Victoria and Albert* and the *Standart* at Reval. Willy was furious: this was yet another intrigue to encircle Germany.

"He aims at war," he scribbled in the margin of a memorandum from Count Paul Metternich, his London ambassador. "I am to begin it, so that he does not get the odium."

The Czar had arranged a surprise for Alexandra. One starry night a tug berthed alongside. The passengers were a famous Russian choir, whose romantic voices enchanted the royal party leaning against the rails. But the enchantment was broken when a Russian aide informed the Queen that "every single singer has been stripped to the skin at the quayside to see if they carried pistols or bombs". On the return voyage the British yacht traversed the Kiel Canal, which during Bismarck's time had been a major reason for Germany's intolerable anti-Danish policy. A regiment of German dragoons drew up at each side of the canal entrance to pay their ruler's respects by escorting the royal voyagers along the waterway. Alexandra had the blinds of her cabin windows pulled down to shut out the repulsive sight. Thus she missed a highly comical instance of royal 'one-upmanship': as the yacht gathered speed the dragoons broke into a canter but were soon outpaced. A disorderly chase ended in chaos. The German officers, puce with indignation, were not slow to report this latest humiliation to their imperial master.

By February 1909 the King's health was giving cause for concern. A persistent chesty cough reduced him to nervous irritability. Relations with Wilhelm had reached rock-bottom. A state visit to Berlin, which offered a forlorn hope of amity, was disastrous from the start. Ignoring his uncle's obvious ill-health, the Kaiser bumptiously organized a military display of unsuitable magnificence. The Germans were sullen and unimpressed. The ceremonial drive to Potsdam almost beggared description. Gaps appeared between the carriages. Willy, driving with Edward, who coughed and smiled, smiled and coughed, cast satanic glances behind him and appeared to be "swearing out loud". In the next carriage Alexandra sat with the Empress Augusta Victoria. Their driver, probably demented by the sight of the trembling spikes of the imperial moustache and the glitter of the ice-cold eyes, lost control. The horses fell down in the traces, tugging the carriage across the road. Alexandra laughed to hide her nervousness. Willy, almost speechless with vexation, thought his aunt was laughing at him. The occupants of the third carriage were unceremoniously tumbled out to make way for the Queen and her niece. The unhorsed coach blocked the road, and as not one Prussian guardsman dared move without orders, spectators pushed it out of the way. Willy vented his spleen on his Master of the Horse, whom he scathingly introduced to the visiting Sovereigns as "the man who made such a fearful bungle with the horses". Thereafter he addressed Alexandra in public as "dear aunt". She retaliated cheerfully with "dear nephew", which left him more annoyed than annoying. These trivia were obscured by an alarming scene at a British embassy dinner when a distressing spasm of coughing sent Edward black in the face. Alexandra loosened his collar, at the same time begging everyone to leave the room except a doctor. Ten minutes later they were called back, to find the King sitting in a rather crumpled collar and resolutely puffing a cigar.

Nothing worked more upon Willy's emotions than the *Entente Cordiale*, which, crowned by Edward's diplomacy in 1904, had ended the Anglo-French feud of centuries. It was in that year that Lady (Walburga) Paget, an ally of Willy's mother in bringing Edward and Alexandra together more than forty years earlier, noted with reservations that the King was much more useful than he had been as Prince of Wales.

"He has a great deal of ability, but is always surrounded by a bevy of Jews and a ring of racing people. He has the same luxurious tastes as the Semites, and same love of pleasure and of comfort. Still, he is a *charmeur* and very able."

Alexandra was not with the King when he visited Paris for the thawing-out prucess, but she loved the 'capital of women' and, although she spoke indifferent French, was devoted to French culture. Once when Sarah Bernhardt played at the London Lyceum the Queen exclaimed to the actress after the performance, "Oh, Madame, how relieved I am to see you alive again after the last act of *La Dame aux Camelias*!" clasping her graceful hands together in a gesture so childlike and spontaneous that Edward bellowed with diuretic laughter.

In February 1907 the King and Queen, travelling as the Duke and Duchess of Lancaster, an incognito as ineffective as that of the Earl and Countess of Munster in an earlier reign, had paid a week's visit to Paris. The Germans followed their social activities with penetrating interest, deciding cynically that this was just another of Edward's efforts to ensure the smooth running of his 'branch establishment'. For the first time Alexandra was able to eat in public restaurants. Her mother, Queen Louise of Denmark, from whom she had inherited her deafness and her will-power, met her there with her youngest sister Thyra. One evening, escorted by a young Danish aide, they were taken to supper in a *separé* or *cabinet particulier*. The aide ordered a *cabinet*. The word *'particulier'* had escaped his memory, and the *maître d'hôtel*, deceived by the urgency of his manner, conducted the party to "an apartment which is known by the word which the aide had uttered". They found themselves in "a highly unexpected place". The chaperon then complicated the situation by saying, '*Non, non . . . Cabinet! Cabinet pour quartre!*" Thereafter he never met Alexandra without blushing.

Frenchmen understood Alexandra perhaps better than the British, who adored her. On her sixty-fifth birthday, the King being abroad, she was in London just before her departure for Sandringham, when she graciously escorted Pierre Loti, a French writer, around the empty staterooms of Buckingham Palace.

"The Queen, with her exquisite hand," he wrote, "unlocked and opened the heavy gilded doors as we passed through the deserted and silent rooms, in all of which, although about to be abandoned, there were clusters of blue hortensias, pink azaleas, orchids and lilies, arranged as if for a *fête*."

He found himself standing before a portrait of Eddy, Duke of Clarence, the Queen's dead eldest son whom she still mourned after seventeen years. "An expression of wonderful tenderness" came over her as she spoke of Eddy. Eventually they arrived in a vestibule overlooking a monumental staircase.

"Her Majesty extended her hand. While I bowed over it she disappeared, and I found myself suddenly quite alone."

Alexandra had clearly mastered the technique of 'the Faery' with which Disraeli so romantically endowed Queen Victoria, who could presumably enter or leave a room before a caller was aware that she had either entered or left.

Other visits abroad, several to Ireland and numerous to Denmark, varied the pattern of Alexandra's life. On her last visit of the reign to Greece a piece of plaster fell from the verandah ceiling of King George's palace and sprinkled her dress with dust. Metaxas was presented to her in Athens. "I am very pleased to meet you," she said. "My brother's house is tumbling to pieces." But the Queen was essentially homekeeping, a jealous mother, an indulgent wife, and she divided most of her reign between London and Sandringham. The great Norfolk estate, which Edward had bought out of Duchy of Cornwall funds amassed by the Consort before his son came of age, was dearest to her because nothing but the ocean separated her from her beloved Denmark. Like Queens before and since, she doted on dogs, but her menagerie at Sandringham also housed doves and horses, bears, tigers, parrots and monkeys. She had some mysterious means of communicating with birds and animals. Some of the pheasants on the estate were known to her by name and approached at her call; and she was extremely cross if they were destroyed by Edward or his undiscriminating guests at shooting parties.

Her taste in dogs verged on the unique. Alec was her champion white Russian wolfhound. Her Japanese spaniels were named Billy and Punchy, a handsome collie Snowball; and there were St. Bernards and Newfoundlands and unusual canines from Tibet and China. In 1908 a beautiful chow, a New Year gift from her equerry, Sir Henry Knollys, arrived after a 12,000-mile journey through China via Yokohama and by steamer to Vancouver Island, thence by train across Canada and by sea to Liverpool. His name was Chum. Dozens of the Queen's dogs won show prizes—bassets like Dido, Madora, Valour, Nero, Vulcan and Warrender. The King was content with one dog at a time;

before his death he lavished affection on Caesar, a wire-haired fox terrier, which slumbered in an easy chair at his bedside and could, like the King, do no wrong. On a journey to Denmark the Queen travelled from Balmoral to join the royal yacht at Dundee, crossing a wide square to the launch with the Lord Provost, a highly mayoral type, who held Caesar's lead. Mill girls cheered the little procession, but the dog, obedient to the calls of nature, decided "to perform the function for which humans thoughtfully provide dogs with lamp posts". Sir William Longair stood patiently holding the lead until Caesar had completed his little prayer, regardless of the hilarity which welled around him. Sir William showed an unexpected sense of humour: he afterwards caused a public water fountain to be erected on the spot.

Alexandra reached the zenith of her career during her nine years as Edward's consort. She is seen at the beginning providing tea in public halls all over London for 10,000 maids of all work, the 'skivvies', the unluckiest and most ill-used of creatures in her view. She is seen defying protocol to send a wreath to the funeral of Cecil Rhodes, who had died under a shadow. She is seen in all her possessiveness excusing her grandchildren offences for which cooler women than 'Darling Motherdear' would have prescribed a good spanking. She doted on the future Duke of Windsor, who at one of the King's parties demanded a ride on the broad shoulders of the tall German diplomat Baron Eckhardstein. The Bishop of London, Dr. Crighton, offered his services. Little David said he would prefer to ride on an elephant, "not on an old giraffe". For this piece of impudence Alexandra banished him in disgrace to the nursery, only to relent and then to fondle him on her lap in a manner which was neither edifying nor useful. She could also inspire deep loyalty, as in the explorer Shackleton, who in 1908 risked his life to plant her standard near the South Pole on a plateau which he named Queen Alexandra's Land.

In that year the Queen's popularity soared. She went to White City to witness the close of the marathon at the first Olympic Games held in London. The gaze of 80,000 spectators was riveted on the dark archway through which the runners would appear. Pietro Dorando of Italy lurched suddenly into the bright July sunlight. After a few yards he fainted and fell, but scrambled to his feet. Twenty yards from the post his legs again gave out, but some friends picked him up. Just then the burly figure of the runner-up, the Stars and Stripes on his vest, came at a loping pace through the arch, gaining rapidly on the exhausted Italian. Dorando, gasping for breath, fell over the line just as the American reached it. The Italian flag went up, only to be pulled down and replaced by Old Glory. Plainly Dorando had finished the course only with the help of his friends. While the crowd wept and roared the Queen was noticed "beating a tattoo on the floor of the stand unrestrainedly with her parasol". The weeping Dorando was led away. Alexandra decided he should have a cup—her personal award—and she presented it to him on the day of the prize-giving "in remembrance of the Marathon Race from Windsor to the Stadium". The act of a 'silly woman', perhaps—but a woman with heart.

Soon the world of Alexandra reeled around her. The death of the King in 1910, the difficult early years of widowhood and of her son George's reign, and the Great War, presaged the end of the old order. Family changes had followed the death of Christian IX in January 1906. He and Queen Victoria had in their different ways dominated the past half-century. Their numerous descendants had spread like the branches of a great oak overshadowing all the other trees in the royal forest. They were the 'grandparents of Europe'. But within five years first Victoria and then Christian were no more and the great tree strained and creaked before the approaching storm.

Always her refuge in trouble, Dagmar followed her father's death with her first visit to Britain for a quarter of a century. Their whispering intimacy, especially 'Aunt Minnie's' conspiratorial little ways, had frequently irritated other members of the Royal Family. A result of this meeting was the joint purchase of an unpretentious white villa at Hvidore overlooking the Baltic near Bernstorff. There they met every year as private persons until the war broke out. Over the drawing-room chimney-piece they engraved a message: "East, West, Home is Best", with their signatures beneath. It was falsely rumoured that the Czar Nicholas had bought Hvidore as a secret retreat to which he could repair after his abdication. He could have done worse.

At Hvidore the magic days of childhood came to mind whenever the sisters met there. Alexandra and her brothers and sisters were born at the Gule (Yellow) Palace on the Amaliegade. With its flaking walls it looked like a neglected *pension*, but the interior sparkled with fresh polish. The owner, Prince Christian of Schleswig-Holstein-Sonderburg-Glucksburg, as he was then, maintained in the eighteen-forties his hyphens and his dignity on a pittance, by royal standards, as a young captain of the King's Guard. Immensely tall, fair, blue-eyed and vigorous, he had every advantage except wealth. His father, Duke Frederick of Schleswig-Holstein, had bred six sons, of whom Christian was the fourth, but the Duke had been impoverished by the Napoleonic war and died leaving the mixed blessings of a declining estate to his eldest son and his other sons to the generosity of relations. Christian fell in love with Louise, King Christian VIII's niece from Hesse-Cassel; by his marriage in 1842 he prepared the way for his ultimate succession to the Danish throne. There stood between him and the crown a swarthy, middle-aged rake, with an aquiline nose and goatee beard, whose leer was usually criticized by those whom he offended. This was Christian VIII's only son and heir, Frederick. Some doubted whether he was the King's son at all, as the King had divorced his mother years before. Frederick had been thrice divorced. His Parisian mistress, Louise Rasmussen, a former grisette, governess and ballet dancer, administered to his needs.

Political and dynastic considerations influenced this interesting Danish version of the 'race for an heir'. Across the foot of Denmark stretched the state of Schleswig and next to it lay Holstein, bordered by Germany. The duchies of Schleswig and Holstein had for centuries been ruled by Oldenburgs, from whom sprang the Danish kings. Over the years the Schleswigers had come to regard themselves as Danes, but the Holsteiners sought independence and looked to the German states for support. The result was the 'festering ulcer' of Schleswig-Holstein. Christian VIII feared that if Frederick died childless and the throne fell vacant a fierce struggle over the duchies would bring in the Great Powers. There were two further complications. One was that a claimant to the Danish throne was another Christian, Duke of Augustenburg (whose daughter was to marry Wilhelm II of Prussia), but his sympathies inclined to the Germans. The Danes considered him a traitor plotting to bring the duchies under German control, and with them the much-prized port of Kiel,

Dagmar ('Minnie') and Alexandra, daughters of King Christian IX of Denmark. Both were destined to marry Emperors. In their youth, as this photograph shows, they looked alike and dressed alike

Alexandra as Princess of Wales with her two sons, Albert Victor (the Duke of Clarence) and the future George V (looking down) and her daughters, the 'whispering Wales sisters'

During her memorable visit with the Prince of Wales to Egypt in 1869 Alexandra not only rode camels but smoked a *huqqah* and ate with her fingers among the ladies of Khedive Ismael's harem

Queen Alexandra was hailed at the coronation of 1902 as the loveliest woman who had ever been crowned in Westminster Abbey

coveted most by Bismarck. The other complication was the old King's daughter Louise, who became Alexandra's mother. As a woman she was subject to the Salic Law (the old custom of the Salian Franks) which barred the succession to a female. King Christian therefore contrived that Louise's mother, who was unacceptable also because of her German husband, should delegate the throne to Louise, and Louise would then hand it to her husband. Eventually when Christian IX became King, the Danes explained: "The King is the Queen." It seemed reasonably fair.

According to Palmerston, only three men ever understood the Schleswig-Holstein problem. One was Prince Albert, but he was dead when Denmark finally lost the duchies to Germany and Austria in 1863. The second was a Danish statesman, but he went off his head. The third was Palmerston himself, but he had forgotten it. Alexandra's lifelong Germanophobia and her antipathy to Wilhem II can be attributed basically to the loss of Schleswig, which enabled the Prussians to build the Kiel Canal as an artery of naval power, vital also to the unity of the German states under Prussia.

All six children of Christian IX and Queen Louise—a tall, capable and self-willed matron in her mature years—were born outside the purple. Frederick, the eldest, was to succeed his father as king in 1906. The second, Alexandra, born on 1st December 1844, was named after an Aunt Alexandra who had first married Louise's brother and then Alexandra II of Russia. There followed between 1845 and 1859 Brother William, who became King of Greece; Dagmar, Russia's future Empress Marie Fedorovna; Sister Thyra; and finally Brother Valdemar. Their father in his youth had entertained ideas much above his station. Christian attended Victoria's coronation as the Danish monarch's envoy. The young Queen cast a friendly eye upon him, but he had scarcely a decent suit of clothes to his back and the Duchess of Kent snubbed him mercilessly; had she not earmarked dearest Albert for her daughter? Later the Queen herself deplored "the fast royal set" in Denmark, notably the preposterous activities of Frederick amid the pimps and harlots and revolutionaries in the pavement cafés of Copenhagen.

So Christian settled down with Louise and reared his six children, compared with Victoria's nine. Louise spoke fluent

7

French and English and strummed the piano with more audacity than accuracy. Her children were instructed in the same subjects. The frugal household swarmed with tutors and governesses. Every day at noon, on his return from the barracks, Captain Christian hailed the four eldest children into the drawing room, threw off his high-collared tunic, and marshalled them through a series of exercises for the arms and legs before launching them into the esoteric mysteries of the somersault and the cartwheel. Alexandra sometimes diverted her friends at Marlborough House by turning cartwheels, explaining that "it is only a matter of speed". She and Dagmar, like Adelaide and Ida before them, shared a spartan bedroom containing two iron bedsteads, a large table and two worn eighteenth-century chairs, with a long shelf for books and toys and a growing collection of photographs on the walls. In this *bourgeois* household the daughters wore home-made frocks.

"I shall bring my children up in sackcloth," Queen Louise explained, "that they may later wear the purple more gracefully."

Rising out of the haze of childhood memories was Rumpenheim, a many-windowed white palace on the Main near Frankfurt. This sylvan refuge belonged to Alexandra's maternal grandfather, the Landgrave of Hesse-Cassel, whose will provided that it should be used for family reunions. Princess Mary, a daughter of George II, withdrew there when her husband the Landgrave became a Roman Catholic: the palace was built to compensate her for this inconsiderate act. Every second year the relations dutifully assembled. The Christians were the shabbiest but the happiest: at one reunion Alexandra's parents had become engaged. Here the Christians could 'live like kings', waited on by other people's liveried servants in an unbroken round of luxury living. Resplendent footmen took the children fishing in the sluggish river, lessons were excused, and Alexandra and her playmates chased one another through corridors and guest rooms, or played 'houses' in the shrubbery. Regular visitors included the Cambridge family from Kew. That Duke of Cambridge who went bride-hunting for his brother William IV had married a Hesse-Cassel, and his son and daughter—George, the future generalissimo of the British Army, and Mary Adelaide, who became Queen Mary's mother—disported among the younger cousins. Alexandra was 3 years old when Mary Adelaide, then 13, first noted her promise of "fairy-like beauty", her immense gusto and an air of command, as she pushed 'little Alexandrine' about in a mailcart. The child was generally known as 'Alix', an affectionate diminutive which lasted her lifetime. Mary Adelaide became almost an elder sister to *la petite Alix*. As George Cambridge spent much of his time in England he regaled his younger cousins with stories of Victoria's life at Windsor. But the Queen intensely disliked large inter-family gatherings and was startled to hear of the boisterous capers at Rumpenheim and later at Fredensborg, the Danish royal palace, where the royals threw each other about at the instigation of the huge Czar Alexander, and the children were allowed to prance up and down on Queen Louise's sofas until they smashed the springs; that sort of thing would never have been condoned at Windsor. Rumpenheim was destroyed by fire bombs during the 1939–45 war; family reunions were then but a faded memory.

Winters at the Yellow Palace and summers at Bernstorff, with Rumpenheim interludes, gave the penny-pinching Christian establishment a choice of reasonable worlds to live in. Copenhageners would watch the family yacht glide from the harbour down the Sound on their way to the white château of Bernstorff in the deer forest. Studies were relaxed, the girls learned from their mother the art of flower arrangement, and Alexandra acquired a superb control of horses from her father. Already the unpunctuality which dogged the princess all her life was becoming obvious. She was invariably late for meals. As a punishment her father ordered her to stand up at the table to drink her coffee, but she never improved. According to one of her biographers, Alexandra's only fault was unpunctuality. Once as Queen she dislocated the whole railway system of North-west Europe by keeping her special train waiting for some hours.

6

Meeting with Edward

MEANWHILE across the North Sea the dilemma of Edward's future haunted Queen Victoria and her German husband, who found his eldest son so unlike himself that he could scarcely believe his ill-fortune. Bertie was a cross that Albert bore to his early grave. Heaven knew he was doing his best for the boy: a strict course of study at the White Lodge in Richmond Park, universities, everything a dutiful heir apparent could possibly desire—everything but an Army career, but that was Bertie's own wish and not to be tolerated. Bertie discouraged the cravings of high-principled tutors to feed his restless mind with knowledge. At 17 he was consequently a grave disappointment to the Prince Consort, who was shocked to think that in another year he would be eligible to reign as king should anything happen to dear Victoria. On the other hand, Von Hohenloe, a future German Chancellor, visiting the palace, was "dismayed by the signs of the prince's nervous awe of his father".

Marriage offered the only solution. But marriage to whom? The prince had already displayed an indiscreet interest in women. Half the eligible German princesses were casting sheep's-eyes at him. The Cambridges had their cottage at Kew, bequeathed to them by George III, and when he was yet 16 Bertie had escaped there from the rigours of Richmond. His glance fell upon a miniature on the mantelpiece. Who was that delightful creature? Mary Adelaide and her mother, the Duchess, went into ecstasies. Did he not know that this was Christian's eldest daughter Alexandra? The prince made some "naïve remarks" and fell upon his dinner. Bertie had seen a copy of this very picture some days earlier when a young friend pulled it from his wallet. The young man was engaged to be married, and the prince assumed that this was his fiancée.

Then only 14, Alexandra had been mentioned as one of the six or eight Protestant princesses upon whom the prince might draw; but she was number five on the list, and German ladies were given precedence. Only *The Times* shrewdly considered Alexandra to be "the most eligible lady". The Queen, however, sustained her prejudice against "the fast Christians"—all those divorces! and that awful King Frederick!—and her son's gaze was deflected from that direction. But the Cambridges were demonstrably persistent match-makers, and they exerted their talents on Alexandra's behalf.

"It would be surprising if we women couldn't arrange this match," wrote the Duchess of Cambridge to the wife of the Danish Minister, Admiral Van Dockum.

The Minister was much impressed. After a call at Bernstorff he exclaimed enthusiastically, "It is impossible that any young man could be unmoved by such unstudied amiability and so much beauty."

On the Grand Tour the Prince saw a Prussian princess in Rome and resolved to remain a bachelor. One thing led to another. In 1860 reports of Alexandra's enchantment, her poise and her grace, filtered back to Windsor. The originator was the Countess Walburga von Hohenthal, the least Prussian of Victoria's maids of honour, who was married to Augustus Paget, the Queen's new Minister to Copenhagen. Walburga's description of the princess as "a half-opened rosebud, so simple and childlike in everything" warmed the Consort's heart. The Pagets were invited to Bertie's nineteenth birthday party at Windsor in November. But Bertie missed the celebrations: he was aboard HMS *Hero*, being buffeted by Atlantic gales after a successful tour of North America. He arrived six days late with tales of his American triumph which his father found incomprehensible. Nothing was said to him, but Lady Paget was ordered to send photographs of Alexandra without telling the Christians. The atmosphere at Windsor so lowered Bertie's spirits that he escaped to his studies at Oxford.

Six months passed. Then the Princess Royal arrived at Osborne. She was called Vicky by her parents and 'Pussy' by her intimates, was her father's treasure—so unlike that Bertie!—and spent much

of her leisure writing to dearest Mamma from Berlin. Behind her
trailed her immense bearded husband 'Fritz' and their frightful
child Willy, who was left with one memory of his grandfather
Albert—being swung by him in a table napkin in the breakfast
room, a harmless exercise in no way comparable to the high jinks
of the Christian Set. 'Pussy' returned to Potsdam to pave the way
for a clandestine meeting between Bertie and Alix. When she saw
the princess she found her the "most fascinating creature in the
world". The Prince of Wales was invited to Germany in September 1861. The Christians were simultaneously lured to Rumpenheim. The prince visited the Duchess of Cambridge at Strelitz,
but he turned pale when his great-aunt urged him to inspect the
nearby cathedral at Speier. Cathedrals depressed Bertie. He did
not really recover his composure until he observed a lady and her
two daughters peering at the relics of bygone bishops in the
chancel. Queen Louise and her children had arrived 'by accident'
from Rumpenheim. After the meeting the Consort wrote to his
Uncle Leopold in Brussels that "the young people seem to have
taken a liking to one another". The Princess fell under the Prince's
fatal spell, which, she was to discover not much later, he cast
upon other women as well. Before she left Rumpenheim she had
concealed a 'photo' of Bertie in her *pelisse*.

Alexandra returned to Denmark and Bertie to his pursuit of
higher education, this time at Cambridge. He had been secretly
warned by the Consort's brother, Duke Ernest of Coburg, against
involvement with Denmark because the Germans would not like
it. Ernest then impudently sent Albert a memorandum written by
a *secretary*! The Consort reacted furiously.

"What is that to you, or what have you to do with it?"

How dare Ernest interfere, when Vicky in Berlin was racking
her dear brain to find a suitable mate for her brother and when
marriage was "morally, socially and politically" in Bertie's
interest? Such a union must not be regarded as a triumph of
Denmark over Britain and Prussia, as Ernest alleged, but as the
blissful outcome of mediation by "our Prussian children", who
deplored the anti-Danish policy of Bismarck and of Fritz's father,
the Emperor William. Having delivered this caveat the Consort a
few months later contracted typhoid, from which he died at
Windsor on 14th December 1861. Mary Adelaide wrote: "Wales
took me to see poor dear Albert. He lay on a small bed in the

Blue Room . . . a wreath of white flowers at his head and single ones laid on his breast and scattered on the white coverlet. With a bursting heart I gazed on those handsome features, more beautiful far than in life, on which death had set so soft a seal that it seemed almost as if he were sleeping. . . . I would have given much to be able to kneel down by the bedside, but there were men in the room."

Victoria blamed her son for the calamity. But dear Albert had so warmly approved of this marriage that the Queen felt in loyal duty bound to give it her blessing. For the present she could not look at the hateful boy without *shuddering*, and in February 1862 he was dispatched with the reliable Dean Stanley on a protracted tour of the Near East, including the Holy Land. Grief-stricken and desolate, the Queen continued the long pilgrimage of life without Albert, and it was not until the summer that she felt strong enough to visit the Beloved One's birthplace. She travelled to Coburg as the Countess of Balmoral, the first of a series of sedate Continental tours which made her a legend abroad. It was arranged that Prince and Princess Christian with Alexandra and Dagmar should meet the Queen at Leopold's palace of Laeken near Brussels. Victoria had been informed that Alexandra "did not look for *anything else* but Love"; the young princess vowed herself to be too unimportant to suit the English—"everybody says they are so solemn". At Laeken the Queen found Alexandra "quite enchanting" and agreed with Uncle Leopold's assessment of her as *un rayon de soleil*. But in the privacy of her boudoir she wept over her own lost happiness. However, it was a great comfort to recall dear Albert's conviction: "We shall be taking the princess—*not her Danish relations!*" and she dried her eyes.

The Prince of Wales plighted his troth in a grotto and gave Alexandra some white heather for luck. Leopold assured Victoria, "All the arguments that one forced him to marry a young lady he had never seen fall most completely to the ground."

After a delay of several days *The Times* was suffered to announce the betrothal in an obscure corner without embellishment, to avoid mortifying the Prussians. A zealous Protestant MP, Mr. Newdegate, asked Lord Palmerston in the Commons to confirm that Alexandra was a Protestant. The old statesman diverted the House with his reply.

"When HM Government considered it their duty to select a

Consort for HRH the Prince of Wales," he began dryly, "certain conditions were laid down as indispensable. She must be young" —this with a half-suppressed smile ('Hear, hear'); "she must be handsome" (loud cheers and cries of 'Bravo!' from the younger Members); "she must be well brought up" ('Hear, hear' and nods of approval from elderly Members); "and finally she must be a Protestant" (delighted uproar).

The Christians made their way back to Denmark slightly vexed by all the humbug. Alexandra could have rejected the heir to the throne of mighty Britain, but the political stakes were too high, not only for them but also for Victoria, who had discovered that Alexander II was seeking Alexandra's hand for the Czarevitch. In one matter, however, the Queen was inflexible. The marriage must not be solemnized in the Chapel Royal at St. James's Palace. There she had married Albert; it was sealed with her grief. The theme of the ceremony was to be Sorrow, so the Abbey and St. Paul's Cathedral were quite out of the question. The Queen chose St. George's Chapel, Windsor, where no member of the royal house had been married since the reign of Edward I. The princess was to submit to one final test: she must spend a month alone with the Queen at Osborne while her fiancé patrolled Italy and the Mediterranean with his new governor, General Knollys.

Much passed in these cloistral confidences at Osborne that can be only surmised, but it seems that the Queen adjured Alexandra not to meddle in politics or to encourage her son to involve himself in Danish affairs—an echo of Uncle Ernest—but always to remember the sensitive feelings of the German relations. Alexandra found the experience 'alarming'. She was also urged to wean Bertie from the cigar habit.

"Beloved Albert so *highly* disapproved of it, which ought to be enough to deter Bertie from it."

Nothing more astonished Alexandra than the spectacle of John Brown leading the melancholy Queen in a pony trap around the grounds. Alexandra might have owed more to his opinion of her than she—or her biographers—ever knew. At all events, the Queen bestowed her benison. Mary Adelaide was entrusted with the supervision of her young cousin's trousseau. Christian came to escort his daughter home for the final leave-taking: he had swallowed his pride by staying at the Danish embassy, an unusual lodging for the future father-in-law of the heir apparent. Busy

months followed. Parliament increased Bertie's income from
£60,000 to £100,000. Alexandra was granted £10,000 a year,
with the promise of another £20,000 should she become a
widow during Victoria's reign. Marlborough House was
renovated exactly as Albert had planned. The Prince of Wales
returned to Windsor in time for the "awful anniversary" of 14th
December when Victoria initiated the macabre practice of usher-
ing the Royal Family into the charnel gloom of the Frogmore
mausoleum where the Beloved One lay at peace. Gifts poured in
from the Courts of Europe. The Danes, with the exception of
pro-German Holstein, voted Alexandra a dowry. Frederick VII
sent with a superb *collier* of pearls the admonition: "Never forget,
Alexandra, that you are a princess of Denmark."

Danish blessings mingled with Danish tears as the young bride,
having been instructed in the rites of the Episcopal Church, set
out for her wedding. A century had passed since a Danish
princess had married abroad. With her travelled her parents,
Brother William—'Veelee'—and Sisters Dagmar and Thyra. She
departed in "one of those natty bonnets which seem to sit better
on her head than anybody else's". The boiler of the steamship
blew up before they left port, and they transferred to another
vessel. After running the gauntlet of Kiel, Altona and Hamburg,
where despite Victoria's foreboding the Germans hailed them with,
Teutonic *furor*, they reached Brussels. Leopold, self-proclaimed
architect of the marriage, embarrassed them with a reception of
absurd magnificence and pressed a bridal gown of Brussels lace
on Alexandra. This had to be refused on Victoria's telegraphed
instructions. Had her uncle not heard of Honiton lace?

The *Victoria and Albert* received the royal party at Antwerp.
At Flushing the crews of HMS *Resistance* and *Warrior* manned the
yards as the royal yacht steamed into the roads. But not a sound,
not a huzzah, not a gun saluted the bridal voyagers. Victoria had
commanded a "noiseless and dignified" reception because of the
Mourning. The townsfolk of Gravesend unpatriotically ignored
this edict. At their first glimpse of Alexandra, who resembled a
slender garden lily in white poplin and bonnet and shawl, the
'solemn' British roared, danced, shed tears of joy. Bertie
arrived late. Alexandra spent the interlude pattering from port
to starboard bowing and waving and blowing kisses to the boat
parties below and the crowds ashore until she was dizzy.

Thousands fell in love with her during that useful interval. Her spirits bubbled. When she went below to change she playfully belaboured 'Veelee' with a parchment scroll of welcome earlier presented to her by the burgesses of Margate. She emerged in mauve Irish poplin, with a cloak of sable-trimmed purple velvet and a white poked bonnet edged with rosebuds. Her crinoline was noticeably unassuming; newspapers hoped this would be a "moderating example" to the ladies of England. Gravesend pier was festooned with orange blossoms and banners proclaiming: "*Velcomen du Udvalgte*" (Welcome, Thou Chosen one). "*Tak, tusind tak,*" she replied. Sixty maids of Kent strew roses in her path to the royal train. The Earl of Caithness at the throttle drove slowly to capture the loyalties all the way to the 'Bricklayers' Arms' in the Old Kent Road, the London terminus so familiar to Adelaide during her uneventful journey forty-five years earlier.

Snow was beginning to fall from a bilious March sky. It presaged trouble. Rivalry between the Lord Chamberlain and the Master of the Horse, and between the Metropolitan and the City police, resulted in a procession far too long for the undermanned forces of law and order. The Mourning further ensured the exclusion of the military, except for a small Lifeguards escort. The crowds were out of hand long before the party reached the City. The Lord Mayor was severed from his Corporation and arrived late and anxious with his crumpled welcome. London Bridge was blocked. Cavalry sabred a passage for the carriages, in the first five of which sat the Christian brother and sisters. The last coach contained the young lovers, faced by the King and Queen of Denmark. Between King William Street and the Mansion House the frightened horses skittered through a heaving lane of hats, umbrellas, crinolines, petticoats, shawls and cloaks.

"Above the cheering," ran a contemporary account, "the shrieks of the women were painfully audible, and boys in a pitiable state of fright were seen waging a battle for life."

One unfortunate lad caught his head in the wheelspokes of the last carriage, but Alexandra "leaned over" and, with her amazing muscular control, disconnected him just in time. Her shoulder was painfully wrenched, but she continued to smile. A terror-stricken mother hurled her baby into one carriage crying, "Look arter him, mister." A dishevelled Danish aide handed over the infant to the police at Paddington. Another baby held up for

Alexandra to see had "all the appearance of being dead". A Lifeguard and his horse crashed to the ground. Casualties collapsed in all directions, some to die. Alexandra's carriage was dragged along remorselessly. Cavalrymen slashed right and left. Helmetless constables were "tossed like gossamer" over the heads of the crowd. Worse calamities were probably averted by Alexandra's insouciance. Eventually the more sanitary spaces of the West End were reached; 30,000 spectators jammed St. James's Street, but were too chilled to demonstrate.

The royal travellers, several hours late, at length flung their frozen bodies into the special train at Paddington. Closed carriages slushed through the driving sleet from Slough to Windsor, where the Queen in her castle, the loyal citizenry, and a squad of Eton schoolboys had waited long hours in vexed anxiety. The cheers of the frostbitten lads apprised the Queen of Alexandra's arrival. Like a "crumpled rose", the princess drooped into the Queen's embrace: "much moved, the Queen kissed her again and again". But after the kissing Victoria felt "desolate and sad" and excused herself from family dinner. Next day, a Sunday, she had recovered sufficiently to show Alix over the Frogmore mausoleum, where she reverentially extolled the virtues of the Beloved One. After this initiation into the inexhaustible religion of Albert-worship Alexandra could do no wrong in the Queen's eyes; if she ever erred the offence was quickly forgotten. Windsor blazed with fireworks on the wedding eve. Only the Queen sat alone in a supernal shroud of memory. Tomorrow she would be more memorable than the bride.

"A great day for old England," chirruped Victoria's cousin George (now Duke of) Cambridge. Not only great but clear and crisp. Frost sparkled in the sunshine. Colours were permitted to be worn for the first time since the Consort's demise, and the wedding guests spilled in bright confusion from the London train; but the Household ladies were limited to greys, mauves and lilacs. The populace wore white silk ribbon rosettes to help the depressed Coventry silk industry, but the guard of honour paraded within the castle courtyard without its band: martial music would have grated on the Beloved One's memory. Catherine of Aragon's box in the chapel was draped in purple velvet and gold. Here sat the Queen, Gartered but otherwise flowing in blackness from head to foot. Many people present had not seen Victoria since the Catastrophe. Fearful glances were cast in her direction, for some believed her to have gone mad, or to be recovering from madness. At the solemn sight Palmerston wept. The Queen's daughters were "quite broke up". Miss Stanley, the Dean's sister, found the Queen "restless, moving her chair, pulling back her long streamers, asking questions of the Duchess of Sutherland. . . . At the first blast of the trumpets she quivered all over and you could see the workings of her face." Only when Mary Adelaide led the princess bridesmaids with Beatrice—'little Bee'—trailing behind did her lips part to reveal the well-known teeth, in a smile which had once reminded a courtier of a friendly badger.

Inevitably Alexandra was late, having taken four hours to dress in the Pink Boudoir next to the chapel. A diamond coronet, the bridegroom's gift, twinkled above the orange blossoms, the lace veil, the bridal gown of white satin and Honiton lace flounces and the train of silver moire. The lovely lace shimmered with a design of rose, shamrock and thistle. She wore Victoria's gift, a bracelet of diamond and opal. Myrtle sprigs from Osborne mingled with the orange blossom, orchid, lily of the valley and white rosebud of the bridal bouquet. The bride seemed to float rather than walk to the altar. Dickens noted her very pale face "full of a sort of awe and wonder . . . the face of no ordinary bride". Thackeray likened the princess and her train of maids to the princesses of the fairy tale who turned into white swans.

"The sun burst forth," Mary Stanley noted, "and it fell on the Queen's cap," as though by some Divine intervention. The organ pealed out the immortal chords of an anthem composed by the versatile Consort, and the Queen "raised her eyes upwards as though transfixed". Jenny Lind, the Swedish Nightingale, sang Albert's Chorale. The Queen's hand went to her heart. Tears washed down her face and she abruptly left the box: there, where the bridal pair stood, she had seen a coffin. She was "affected much", especially as Bertie, in his scarlet uniform, kept looking up at her with "an anxious clinging look, which touched me much". The Archbishop's voice broke the anxious silence, and the Queen returned. However, the Canterbury exhortation was drowned by the premature tuning-up of the orchestra, and Alexandra tittered nervously.

"The Danish princess has made Danes of us all," whispered

Palmerston, echoing another guest, dear Alfred Tennyson, who had hailed the Sea King's daughter from over the sea—"we are all of us Danes in our welcome to Thee". Disraeli declared that this was the only pageant which had not disappointed him. Little Willy, the bridegroom's nephew, then 4 years old and dressed as a Highlander, finding the knees of Edwards' small kilted brothers, Uncles Arthur and Leopold, much to his taste, nibbled them continuously and, when he tired of the flavour, pinched their bottoms. He also distinguished himself by tossing an aunt's muff into the public road. Dear Willy!

Alexandra dropped a curtsey to the Queen as she repeated the marriage vows. Guns fired when Bertie placed the wedding ring on her finger: the jewelled motif spelled out his initials. Each blank shot seemed to pierce the Queen. "Ah, dear brother," she wrote to the King of Prussia, "what a sad dismal ceremony it was!" Her present "numbed existence" was no life at all, and it was hard to watch the children of her "angel of a husband" starting off on their own lives "when one feels so utterly dead oneself". However, Albert's longfelt desire had been fulfilled and she was content.

Turbulent scenes followed the departure of the bride and bridegroom for the honeymoon at Osborne. A plebeian mob had swarmed into Windsor in the wake of the Quality from London. Now began a mad race to catch the next train home. Guests were caught up in a fantastic *mêlée* as they tried to find their carriages. Episcopal hats, torn coats, crushed bonnets, scattered ribbons and diamonds, torn epaulettes and crumpled velvets and crinolines milled together in hopeless confusion. The Archbishop reached Slough station only by hanging desperately to the back of someone's coach. Dukes and duchesses were crushed together with pickpurses, navvies and grocers in the ceremonial train. Miss Stanley, finding herself locked in the station lobby for half an hour, finally escaped by cracking the window with her umbrella.

7

The Elephant Man

MARRIAGE to the Prince of Wales—'my little Man'—opened up for Alexandra an exotic life compared with the haphazard informalities of the Danish Court. A month after the wedding she was exploring Sandringham. Once she lost the way and begged a lift from a passing waggoner. Hodge cast a sour eye on the princess and her lady-in-waiting. He had been drawing dung—"and I caunt have wimmin bringing their petticoats into my cart". Now Alexandra understood why the British were 'solemn'. This little scene merely underlined the contrasts in her new existence, for soon she was transported into the great world of fashion as Bertie, in a series of post-marital progresses through the provinces and Scotland, interspered with a round of festivities in London, proudly showed off his bride.

Her love was a silken thread enchaining a bridegroom whose surly outbursts of temper, especially when she was late for engagements, subsided before her invincible sweetness. Edward was an ardent and purposeful lover, and by the summer of 1863 Alexandra was preparing for the birth of her first child the following March. Elaborate arrangements for the lying-in were made at Marlborough House, but in the afternoon of 8th January 1864 the princess went into labour in a sleigh on the ice at Frogmore while Edward and his friends were playing hockey. Three hours later she gave birth to a son and heir. Not a stitch of baby clothing, not a crib, not a nurse was available. Only the Windsor physician, Dr. Brown, was at hand and he, with Lady Macclesfield, an experienced matron who had borne a dozen children, brought into the world Prince Albert Victor, afterwards Duke of Clarence. He was named Victor after his godmother the Queen and was the first of her descendants to assume the celestial name of his grandfather the Consort. He was given the additional names of Christian after his other grandsire and Edward after his father.

That autumn the family travelled to Denmark, the first of some forty trips Alexandra made to the homeland before the Accession. Incredible and violent changes had occurred. Christian and Louise had ascended the throne, which reeled under the shock of the war with Germany and Austria and the subsequent loss of the Schleswig-Holstein duchies. "This horrible war," said Edward, "will be a stain for ever on Prussian history"; it was also a stain on British honour, which sacrificed Denmark to British self-interest. Family harmony was shattered by the conflict and increased the asperity of Victoria's relations with her son. Alexandra could do little for her father except demonstrate her displeasure. When the royal yacht entered Schleswig-Holstein waters the Prussian flag was hoisted at the yardarm. The Princess ordered its removal. Let no one preach to her about protocol. "I will not move one step until it is down." And down it came.

Other changes were happier. 'Veelee' had become King of Greece in 1863, Dagmar was betrothed to the Czarevitch Nicholas, and Frederick was affianced to Princess Louise, the Swedish King's only daughter. Frederick, a former Oxford undergraduate, had entertained amorous feelings for Edward's sister Helena, but Victoria intended her to marry a German; the Danish Crown Prince's emotions were "of no consequence" to her. Christian swallowed his fury.

"They wound our most sacred feelings," he complained. "That is typically English. They think of nothing but their own advantage and never consult their heart."

Bitterness lingered still when the Wales family reached Copenhagen. The visitors called on the Swedish royals in Stockholm, leaving Victor Albert with the Christians at Bernstorff. This came to the ears of Victoria, who, on the basis of a legal ruling in the reign of George II, held that she had the right to stop any young successor being taken out of England. She telegraphed angrily demanding that the child be sent to her in Scotland at once. The message was fortunately garbled in transmission and no action was taken.

Soon Alexandra was pregnant again, and George Frederick

Ernest Albert, the future George V, was born at Marlborough House on 3rd June 1865. Fire broke out above the royal nursery a few days later. Edward tore off his jacket, hacked up floorboards, flooded the nursery and the main staircase, injured a knee in the process, but saved all. The next accouchement brought unguessed anguish. On 14th February 1867 the Princess of Wales took to her bed with acute rheumatism and a high fever. The future Princess Royal (Louise) was born six days later. The rheumatism concentrated in the right knee joint. Rheumatic fever then often proved fatal. A medical conspiracy of silence heightened public fears. All Alexandra's engagements for the year were cancelled. Alarm, such as had not been felt since the calamity of Princess Charlotte, swept the country when the Christians arrived and Victoria interrupted the Mourning at Windsor to visit the patient.

"You must not speak of dying, Alix dear," said the Queen. "You have brought us nothing but good since you came amongst us, and we cannot spare you."

Recovery was slow and painful. *The Lancet* revealed that for some time she would have to use a mechanical support. Alexandra was dosed with opiates and laid upon a hop bed. She was bedridden for four months. The disease left her with a halting gait and a permanent limp. Fashionable women incredibly simulated 'the Alexandra limp' and wore bustles to create the impression of stooping, just as they sported the celebrated 'dog-collar' with which Alexandra hid an early operation scar—astonishing examples of sycophancy probably unparalleled since the king who wore no clothes.

Alexandra's lifelong interest in hospitals dated from this time. Hospitals had been considered unfit for ladies to visit. The first to be patronized was St. Bartholomew's. Wards, beds and wings were named after her nearly everywhere. But it was the Merrick affair which set Alexandra apart from other women of rank. There was discovered in the waiting-room of Liverpool Street railway station a human monster of the most repugnant appearance. Passengers who entered left feeling suddenly ill. Women fainted at the sight. The ghastly creature, huddling in a corner like an animal, had a trunk of flesh, coarse and grey like an elephant's: he was dumb with terror and distress. One traveller bolder than the rest found that this was John Merrick. In his pocket was a card bearing the name of the great London healer, Sir Frederick Treves.

With her grandchildren in 1904. The photograph shows Prince
George, the future Duke of Kent, in her arms; then (from left to
right) Prince Henry (the Duke of Gloucester), Princess Alexandra
of Fife, Prince Albert (afterwards George VI), Princess Maud of
Fife (who married Lord Carnegie), the Prince of Wales (afterwards
Edward VIII) and Princess Mary (Princess Royal)

A family portrait of 1907. From left to right: the Queen of Portugal,
King Edward VII, the Empress 'Dona' of Germany and her
husband, Kaiser Wilhelm II, Queen Alexandra, the Queen of Spain
and her husband King Alfonso XIII of Spain, and Queen Maud

(*Left*) One of the last photographs of King Edward and Queen Alexandra taken aboard the Royal yacht at Cowes in 1909. (*Below*) Visiting war wounded. Queen Alexandra as Queen Mother visits the hospital named after her at Roehampton

The famous man hurried to the station. At the sight of him Merrick broke hoarsely into speech. Two years earlier Treves had found Merrick to be a rare advanced case of elephantiasis. But he had since been carried around Continental fairgrounds on exhibition until he ceased to pay for his keep, was callously abandoned and shipped home. The doctor took him to the London Hospital, where Alexandra demanded to see the Elephant Man. Brushing aside protests—"I go!"—she limped into the cubicle where Merrick was screened off from more normal patients. She shook his hand and sat by his bedside smiling and chatting away, and in a few minutes did more to restore the man's self-respect than all the doctors and nurses combined. Thereafter she often called on him, realizing that his physical condition had affected his mind and that the presence of another human being who believed in him would help restore his mental balance. She sent him Christmas cards and gifts, including a signed photograph, which he would let no one touch: he clasped it to his chest and rocked himself with emotion. Little could be done to cure the skin complaint, but in his last days he became rational. Whatever else may be written about this unique princess, the cases of Merrick and Dorando unchallengeably distinguished her from others of her sex as a woman of practical Christian piety.

Autumn found Alexandra almost fully recovered—"sitting like a swan" in her barouche. A fourth child was on the way, and in July 1868 she gave birth to Princess Victoria, who lived until 1935 but never married, to the end the inseparable companion and confidante of George V. There were no complications this time, and plans were laid for a prolonged holiday visit, mixed with business, to Europe and the Near East. First Alexandra wished to show the three elder children to their grandparents in Denmark, but again Victoria complained that the "children *of* the country" should not be taken *out of* the country but should be left with her. Edward, although he was now being talked about as 'Prince Hal' because of his dubious associations, loyally supported his wife and the Queen yielded.

After a brief stay with Napoleon III and the Empress Eugenie the Wales family spent six weeks in Denmark, after which the children were returned to England while Edward and Alexandra went on to Berlin and thence to Vienna, where she bloomed like

8

a rose under the genial influence of the Emperor Franz-Josef. Soon she was immersed in the splendours of the Orient. By February 1869 the Khedive Ismael was welcoming them to the prodigious Esbekieh Palace, the state bedroom of which was luxuriously equipped with solid silver beds worth £3,000 apiece and the furniture veneered with beaten gold. The room was so vast that "even when the candles were lit there might be somebody sitting at the other end without your knowing it".

Six weeks melted away on the Nile, permitting Edward to bang away at hyena, duck and crocodile, while Alexandra smoked the *huqqah*, sometimes dined with the harem ladies ("disgusting", said her lady-in-waiting), inspected cataract, catacomb and cave, the Pyramids of Gizeh and the Sphinx, indefatigably riding on a white ass caparisoned in red and gold velvet. She left an indelible impression on the susceptible Egyptians, and even more on the Turks. The visitors crossed to Istanbul improbably as 'Mr. and Mrs. Williams', and the Sultan courted the displeasure of Allah by offering his arm to Alexandra, a unique distinction for a Christian woman. The party thence proceeded to the Crimea, where Edward, reproducing the enthusiasm of his great-uncle William IV for historic battlefields, scanned Sebastopol, the Alma and Balaclava with his glass. Finally they carried out what became an Alexandrine ritual—a visit to 'Veelee' and his Queen Olga.

The saucy seventies succeeded the sedate sixties and brought to full flower the Marlbocracy, the Marlborough House Set. The doors of the red brick mansion in The Mall were thrown open to rich or talented celebrities from the middle and upper strata of Society whose main preoccupation was to please the heir to the throne and divert his mind from the funereal atmosphere of Windsor, Osborne and Balmoral. The millionaire Rothschilds, who between them owned the Vale of Aylesbury and provided the funds with which Britain purchased the Suez Canal, dined under the dazzling chandeliers with poets, diplomats, philosophers, gamblers, artists, authors, courtesans, American heiresses who intended to marry into the peerage and a galaxy of rich or exceptional people. The association with the Rothschilds—Natty, Leo and Alfred, who had been at Cambridge with Edward, and Ferdy, head of the Austrian branch of the family banking concern —received unfavourable publicity. Court officials wrung their hands, fearing that national secrets would be confided to a commercial firm. In fact the Prince, deprived of access to state documents, often received official news from his Jewish friends long before his mother's ambassadors and Ministers. Jews the world over, who suffered crippling disabilities, gloried in the royal favour bestowed upon the grandsons of a ghetto apprentice: a London rabbi remarked that although their Messiah had not yet arrived the Jews certainly had their Holy Family.

At the dawn of this era Alexandra gave birth to her fifth child and third daughter, Maud Charlotte Mary Victoria, later Queen of Norway. Joy quickly turned to anxiety, for it was precisely at this time that a time-bomb went up under the Marlborough House Set. Sir Charles Mordaunt filed a petition for divorce, citing two of the Prince's friends, Lord Cole and Sir Frederick Johnstone. Insanity was alleged against Lady Mordaunt, who was 23, but Edward had visited her, had written her incriminating letters, and he was served with a subpoena. During this fresh crisis Alexandra outwardly condemned the scandal-mongering and protested Edward's innocence, as did the Queen. But inwardly she was distressed and humiliated, and privately the Queen deplored the profligacy of a high-living *caste* whose dreadful example to the lower orders could but involve the monarchy in obloquy and encourage latent forces of republicanism. The Cambridge ladies at Kew durst not speak of the affair, they were so shocked. Alexandra after seven years of married life knew enough to be sure that if her husband was not exactly innocent of 'undue familiarity' with Mordaunt's wife he was not wholly guilty. She firmly advised against a plea of royal immunity; Edward must give evidence in open court. He was 28. During seven sweating minutes in the witness-box he denied adultery. But in the clubs and the pubs the snobocracy called him 'Teddy' and he was hissed in the streets; apparently his chief crime was to have been found out. He fled to the Amphytrion Club, where Alfred Rothschild lulled him with piano music through a sleepless night.

The wound cut deep. Alexandra, after a brief cry into the bosom of the German-born Duchess of Manchester, departed to Denmark. The estrangement was ended by the Franco-Prussian War. Victoria, fearing that if the Germans invaded Denmark they might carry her off, ordered her back. Edward, who travelled to

Copenhagen to escort Alexandra home and earn her pardon, hoped the Prussians would get a thorough beating, but when the question of helping Napoleon III arose, the Duke of Cambridge asked, 'What the hell can we do without an army?" The Napoleons settled at Chislehurst. The Waleses took the Prince Imperial under their wing and mourned him deeply when a spear carried him off in the Zulu War. The tragedy stimulated in Edward those Gallic sympathies which finally impelled him towards the *Entente Cordiale*. How different was 'Pussy's' attitude!

"Marvellous!" she gloated when Paris was bombed. "Gay and charming Paris! What mischief that loose Court had done to English Society, what harm to the young and brilliant aristocracy of England!"

The Mordaunt case should have proved a warning to the Prince of Wales but, danger passed, he "chased the glowing hours with flying feet". His life became "a perpetual search in daytime for hours he had lost at night", in gambling clubs, at brilliant parties after the races, at country houses. Attractive women were honoured by his attentions. 'Skittles', the notorious Catherine Walters, whose language was 'a caution', lured him to tea parties and baccarat sessions at her Mayfair clubs. The Prince varied these amusements sometimes by flushing the kidneys at French and German spas or filling the lungs with ozone at Cowes, where Alexandra, in a neat white serge suit and nautical cap, paced *Osborne*'s deck as though she had not a care in the world.

Her last refuge was 'dear old Sandringham', but even there her domesticity was invaded by assorted house guests. Reverend gentlemen from Norfolk parishes played for a penny a point while Edward chain-smoked cigars and made the vicars cough. If Adelaide had her Howe, Alexandra had her Sir Dighton Probyn, V.C., who had joined the Household as comptroller and treasurer when he was 39. Probyn adored, even worshipped, Alexandra to the end of her life, by which time he had acquired the air of a patriarch with his upright, ascetic figure and flowing white beard. To him she was 'The Beloved Lady'. If she mounted her carriage, Sir Dighton was there to hand her safely aboard. At church he conducted her to the pew. If she took snapshots, Sir Dighton set the camera. The perfect courtier was matched by the perfect secretary-companion, Charlotte Knollys, the spinster daughter of the general and the sister of Francis, the Prince's private secretary. Charlotte sometimes wrote as many as sixty letters a day in the royal service.

Gossips could never fault these two stalwarts, but the friendship of Alexandra with Oliver Montagu of the House of Sandwich, appeared to be on a different plane. Montagu loved her, although she bore towards him no more than affectionate gratitude. Edward's frequent absences threw them much together, perhaps not always to discuss religion, although it was probably a spiritual bond which united them. History is rich in cavaliers whose favoured position at Court inspired the jealous chatter of less privileged courtiers, who then babbled to the Burneys, the Creeveys and the Grevilles of their day. Edward in his unquenchable thirst for novelty neglected Alexandra atrociously, but she found solace in her children and in the pursuits of rural life. Yet when in 1875 the Prince departed for India she genuinely pined. Her insistence on going with him had been rebuffed by the Queen. Mary Adelaide said, "Though I am *quite* in favour of Wales going to India, I grieve for her at the long separation." Another friend found her looking "inexpressibly sad". Against the Queen's renewed opposition she took the children to Denmark. At last Edward was home again with strange Eastern presents for the family, and they resumed the old routine; but as her duties increased Alexandra's vagueness grew, irritating Edward but sometimes producing comic effects. At a dinner party she once sat between a dachshund breeder and a carnation cultivator. She mixed them up. When the dog man was talking she thought he was the flower lover.

"Yes," she said sweetly, "that kind are nice, but personally I like best of all the old-fashioned, fat, pink ones—and they smell so lovely!"

Edward also had his moments. An unfortunate waiter once splashed spinach over his shirt front. He rose up with an oath, grabbed a handful of spinach and rubbed it into his chest declaring, "Well, I might as well make a complete mess of it," and strode out in a rage. A favoured visitor to Marlborough House was the poet laureate, creator of the banal ode of welcome on Alexandra's arrival in Britain. While he was reading it to her, at her request, the Princess shrieked with laughter. *Punch* parodied the ode in 1873 when Alexandra Palace was built. A string of witty verses in the Bard's style ended: "Cricketers, Archers, or

Foresters we, Tory or Whig, or whatever we be, We are all of us happy to welcome thee—'Alexandra'!" Another 'pet' was Gladstone. Unlike the Queen, who bridled whenever the hateful 'firebrand's' name was mentioned, Alexandra discovered his deep spiritual qualities. To Alexandra, who read a chapter of the Bible every day, he was "a dear man", and she told Mrs. Gladstone: "You don't want your William to be called anything but Mr. Gladstone. You don't care about names and titles and orders. When I think how people trouble and struggle about these things, and what dreadful persons get them, I cannot understand it at all."

On Gladstone's death she wrote to his widow noting that "his longing and wish to go to his heavenly home were granted to him on the very day of our Saviour's Ascension".

A sparkling newcomer at this time was Lillie Langtry. The Jersey Lily with her aureole of golden hair and her hypnotic eye so charmed the London crowds when she rode with Edward in Rotten Row that people battered each other with their umbrellas to get a better view. The Lily was poisoned by an oyster at Marlborough House. The Princess sent her home, called next day, begged her to lie down and made her tea. Lord Charles Beresford—'my little Rascal'—was another glittering figure on the Marlbocratic merry-go-round, a *farceur* of considerable ingenuity. Once at Sandringham he doped a cock and placed it under the bed of a pompous guest, who was startled out of a deep sleep when the outraged fowl "greeted the rising sun from an unaccustomed position" in the chamber pot. His pranksome rival was the Prince Imperial. He and the royal hosts attended a *seance* at Mrs. Cust's waterfront cottage at Cowes. Furniture suddenly began to dance and Alexandra felt "angel's wings" brushing her cheeks. The lights went up to reveal Beresford in stockinged feet sprinkling the company with flour. Edward entered into the spirit of the occasion and he and Louis Napoleon hauled a live donkey up through the window of a guest room at Mrs. Cust's and put the beast to bed. He had a more injurious experience at Jimmy de Rothschild's manor in Buckinghamshire. Visitors are still shown the banister down which the Prince of Wales slid and fractured a kneecap.

Alexandra had come to accept her husband's irregularities with resignation. Religion was her refuge. On 6th April 1871 a third son, her sixth child, was born at Sandringham. There was

just time to christen him Alexander John Charles Albert before
he expired. She marked his grave with a white cross inscribed:
"Suffer little children to come unto Me". He was the first English
prince to be named John since Henry IV's reign; the name, and
the tragedy, were to be repeated in the next century when Queen
Mary lost her youngest son. This bereavement, and the heartache
of the Mordaunt case, were followed by the terror of Edward's
typhoid attack in November. In thanksgiving for his recovery
the Princess presented a brass lectern to Sandringham church
with the text: "When I was in trouble I called upon the Lord,
and He heard me." The "universal feeling" of the public during
those "painful, terrible days" prompted the Queen to express her
"deep sense of the touching sympathy of the whole Nation",
although she opposed any further public demonstration as an
unnecessary "show". Nevertheless 14,000 people joined in
singing "Thou hast not given me over to death" at a St. Paul's
thanksgiving service. A spectator opened his mouth so wide in
astonishment at the crowds that he dislocated his jaws, according
to *The Lancet*. It is generally accepted that republicanism died in
Britain with Edward's recovery.

8

The Willy Problem

THE NEXT two decades up to the accession blossomed with
beautiful women, among whom reigned the Duchess of Leinster
and her sister Lady Helen Vincent, the Lady Londonderry of her
day, Lady Ermonde, Mrs. Cornwallis-West and the Countess of
Warwick ('Darling Daisy'). But Margot Asquith was moved to
observe that Alexandra made even this array of the fair "look
common". Whisperings, as Lord Esher loyally described them,
were inevitable; but Alexandra refused to allow Edward's
infidelities to defile their basic friendship. Queen Victoria would
have 'died' had she heard her son questioning an old lady who,
in Albert's lifetime, had been expelled from Court for trying to
flirt with the Consort.

"After all," she explained, "the Coburgs inherited a roving eye.
How humiliating for a man to think that no woman ever wanted
to flirt with him!"

"I doubt," said Edward, "if that is a form of humiliation on
which either you or I could pose as an authority."

In Alexandra's presence people were encouraged to discuss
things, not individuals; she probably dreaded what she might
hear. What pleased her genuinely was praise of her husband's
diplomacy from sages such as Gladstone and Disraeli. Both
statesmen blamed his shortcomings on the Queen's unapproach-
able grandeur: with the death of John Brown her eyes were more
than ever raised upwards and she acquired those 'faery' qualities
which imbued her from the Jubilee to her death. Edward, plump,
middle-aged, rakish, occasionally burst forth in rages of frustra-
tion. Although he could often equal diplomats at their arcane

freemasonry, he yearned, as had George IV before him, to become
a great general, and was mortified when the Queen and the
Government refused him the leadership of the Brigade of Guards
during the Arabi Pasha rebellion in Egypt. Now Willy, too, began
to irk him sadly. In the autumn of 1880 the future Emperor, at
21, had become engaged to 'Dona' of Augustenberg. At Sandringham—unlucky Sandringham—he invoked his uncle's wrath by
'taking him up'. Edward called him a 'puppy'. Willy in his Junkers
arrogance was already treating his mother as an *Englanderin*
who tried to run Germany to the orders of the Queen and his
detested uncle. Actually he hated his mother and despised the
British Royal Family except the Queen. Two days before Edward's
birthday Willy flounced back to Berlin. For the sake of peace the
Prince of Wales attended his wedding the following February,
but Alexandra stayed home.

A month later the Russian Emperor Alexander II was blown up
by a bomb after a military review in St. Petersburg. Overruling
the fears of Victoria, the Prince and Princess of Wales attended
the funeral. Brother-in-law 'Sacha' had now become Alexander III
and Dagmar reigned as the Empress Marie Fedorovna. The contrast between the life of 'the Waleskis', as they were called, and
their Russian relations was overwhelming. In Britain 30 per cent
of the people were living below the poverty line, but even
their conditions were idyllic compared with the Russian
peasants'. A heavy, threatening atmosphere brooded over St.
Petersburg.

"We can only guarantee your safety," the chief of police told
the British visitors, "if you keep away from the Czar and Czarina."

They were isolated from the Russian Court. Sacha and Dagmar
were confined to the Anitchkoff Palace where a narrow backyard
"worse than a London slum" was sealed off for open-air exercise.
When eventually the visiting royals relaxed in the Crimea their
villa at Livadia needed a small army to guard it. Alexander
proved to be a weak ruler, hectored by a purposeful wife. History
continues to point to the two sisters—Alexandra with her
ancestral distrust of the Germans and Dagmar in her hard shell
of conservatism—as contributory causes of the 1914–18 war and
the destruction of the Romanovs.

The 'Willy problem' continued to distort relations between the
Saxe-Coburgs and the Hohenzollerns. When Edward visited

Berlin for his sister's silver wedding in 1883—again without Alexandra—he found his nephew strutting in Royal Stuart tartan, his grandmother's gift. His moustaches were beginning to dart upwards and he was giving away portraits of himself in Highland attire with the words "I bide my time" written beneath: it was one of the few 'photos' which Alexandra did not add to her heterogeneous collection. The Prince was again in the Prussian capital for the eighty-eighth birthday, and later the funeral, of Willy's grandfather William I. Now Willy was intriguing with the Czar, to whom he represented his uncle as "the most formidable foe of Russia". Dagmar dutifully divulged these diplomatic ploys in letters to Alexandra.

Troubles nearer home temporarily obscured the 'Willy problem'. The assassination of Lord Frederick Cavendish and Mr. Burke in Phoenix Park were still an evil memory when in the spring of 1885 the Prince and Princess of Wales paid their second state visit to Ireland in seven years. Edward was the more determined to go because the Fenians had placed a derisory figure of £2,000 on his head, dead or alive. Fenian bomb outrages failed to deter him. He brusquely dispensed with police escorts wherever possible. The sturdy Dubliners expressed their loyalty by smashing windows and rioting, but Alexandra's smile "did all that could be expected of it". She inspected hovels. She was made an honorary Doctor of Music of Dublin University. Nationalists in Cork jigged with rage at these unseemly displays of sycophancy in Dublin and threatened reprisals. Victoria ordered the route to Cork to be changed, but the telegram went astray. Before they reached Mallow the royal party were greeted with black flags emblazoned with the skull and crossbones, stones rattled against the railway carriage windows, fists were shaken, the royal path strewn with curses, and at Mallow station, to which they were pursued by jaunting-cars, a surging mass met them with two empty miniature coffins. One was hurled towards the Princess and almost struck her, but a young officer (a few years earlier Alexandra had shown him how to cure warts) spurred his horse into the crowd and the royal coach sailed on unharmed. Alexandra was the soul of courageous resolution throughout the tour, never quite realizing how close to death she had been.

How safe was the monarchy? The answer came with Victoria's Jubilee in 1887. From the heights of Parnassus the Queen airily vetoed every proposal that she should change her saintly mourning weeds for state robes at the Abbey ceremony. Alexandra was sent to reason with her, but left the audience after receiving "the snub of my life". The Queen had been Empress of India since 1875. The heir apparent had not entirely approved of this apotheosis. He himself had vehemently refused to be styled 'Imperial Highness', for the change took place while he was in India, where he had severely admonished British officers for calling Indians 'niggers'. But the nation and the Empire worshipped Victoria as the indestructible arbitress of their fate, the poor and the ill-used along with the high and mighty.

Left to his own devices Willy, the dedicated grandson, would no doubt have organized the Jubilee, as he later contrived to 'boss' so many of his English relations' public festivals. But Willy was more fruitfully engaged. With the aid of Bismarck and his son Herbert he was trying to prove that his father was unfit to ascend the throne. Frederick was still Crown Prince at the time of the Jubilee. He was in the grip of throat cancer, but it was he, not Willy, who headed the procession of foreign potentates behind the Queen's carriage—"a giant Wagnerian figure on a high-stepping black charger". The brazen helmet, surmounted by a brass eagle, flashed in the June sunlight. Yet the spreading golden beard and the dazzling white uniform failed to stir British breasts. The crowd stopped cheering when he approached and resumed only after he had passed. True liberal though he might be, as monarchs went, his condition dismayed the guests at a golden gathering at Marlborough House, for the strangled splutter which emanated from the struggling lips horrified all who heard it. He would be the first of those present to meet with a disagreeable death; the other two were Crown Prince Rudolph of Austria-Hungary, who was to commit suicide at Mayerling, and George of Greece, marked down for murder. Alexandra always hoped that when 'Fritz' reigned at Potsdam the lost duchies would be restored to Denmark. But after three months in England desperately seeking a cure he retired to San Remo, where his wife enraged the Germans by summoning the unfortunate Scottish specialist Mackenzie, whose disputed diagnosis is one of the mysteries of medical history. Willy distinguished himself by visiting his father once at the Villa Zirio, treating him as though he were already defunct, and abusing his English mother on the doorstep.

The old Kaiser Wilhelm's death in March 1888 coincided with Alexandra's silver wedding. At a family party Victoria found her daughter-in-law looking "lovely in grey and white, more like a bride just married than a silver wedding one of twenty-five years". Alexandra refused to attend the old Emperor's funeral—he was "the thief who stole Schleswig-Holstein"; but when his son died after a harrowing reign of ninety-nine days she accompanied Edward to Berlin because she thought 'Pussy' would need all her womanly sympathy, which she most certainly did. Willy on ascending the Imperial throne made his mother virtually a prisoner, acting on the impulsive notion that she had been smuggling state papers to London. He then consigned his father to the grave with almost indecent haste. The coffin, according to Emil Ludwig, stood on its bier among hammering workmen "like a tool-chest". Alexandra was appalled by the lack of reverence. Clergymen "rattled away" as at some conventicle, while Field-Marshal Blumenthal reeled about gossiping with the Standard drooping over his shoulder.

Driving to Potsdam after the obsequies, Alexandra declared: "Willy is *mad*!" Ably abetted by Herbert Bismarck, who had called Willy's father "a dumb man unfit to rule", the new emperor sneered at his mother and his dead father's memory and assumed patronizing airs which reduced Edward to a passion when he recalled that black day. One of Willy's first acts of statesmanship was to write to Victoria that he meant to visit the Czar and Franz-Josef—"We Emperors must stand together"—and complaining that Edward and Alexandra had taken him amiss and were not to be trusted. His widowed mother's doleful appearance at Windsor opened the floodgates. Marie Mallet, the Queen's maid of honour, found her listless and draped in crêpe, her face invisible. The "poor thing" was trembling with grief.

"Her cup of sorrow is terribly full and this place must be so full of happy memories. Now all turns to pain."

The malevolent shadow of Wilhelm II continued to pursue his uncle and aunt. The All Highest in his ostentatious white and gilt steam yacht *Hohenzollern* sailed to Cowes during the early nineties. Queen Victoria made him an honorary Admiral of the Fleet. He chortled, "Fancy wearing the same uniform as Nelson!" As relief from her insufferable nephew Alexandra immersed herself in preparations for the wedding of her daughter Louise to the

Duke of Fife, but in the midst of these activities the Shah of
Persia arrived. The occupant of the Peacock Throne cast an un-
favouring eye upon the ladies-in-waiting, most of them middle-
aged and all very staid.

"These are your wifes?" he asked Edward incredulously. "They
are old and ugly. Have them beheaded and take new and pretty
ones."

By 1890 the antipathy between Edward and Wilhelm was
developing into an enmity which Ludwig thought would "affect
the history of the world". The Kaiser called his uncle "the old
Peacock" and to Edward he was "The Boss of Cowes" and "the
most brilliant failure in history". In front of Alexandra her
nephew scolded Edward like a schoolboy. Even the indulgent
Queen described her grandson as "an impetuous and conceited
youth". He was 37 then. The Emperor rubbed salt into Edward's
wounds when war threatened between Russia and Britain on the
north-west frontier of India.

"Well, now you can go to India," he said, "and show whether
you're any good as a soldier."

He further endeared himself by calling his uncle "the only
Crown Prince in Europe who has not seen active service", and
he mortified his aunt when in a speech at Frankfurt he declared
that Germany "would rather sacrifice forty-two millions of
inhabitants on the field of battle than surrender a single stone"
of Schleswig-Holstein.

Home patterns in the nineties reproduced those of earlier decades:
Edward racing and gambling and dallying with Amaryllis in the
shade; Alexandra, neglected and unhappy, finding solace in
jealously-guarded domesticity; warnings in which the Princess
saw the hand of God but which Edward ignored once danger was
past. Under the heading "The Prince in Trouble" his brilliant
biographer, Sir Philip Magnus, has written a graphic account of
the Tranby Croft affair, which discoloured the Prince's reputation
in the summer of 1891. Tranby Croft was a mansion near Doncas-
ter, where Edward played baccarat with counters, decorated with
his plumed badge, which he carried from one country-house
gaming table to another "as a Turk carried his prayer mat". One
of the players was caught cheating, and at the subsequent trial
in June before Lord Chief Justice Coleridge the Prince was

subpoenaed to give evidence—"dragged", in his mother's words, "through the dirt". While Edward was being denounced as a vicious gambler and many foreigners thought it was the Prince who had been caught with the cards up his sleeve, Alexandra maintained an impenetrable composure. But in private she upbraided him with the considerable vigour of outraged motherhood, indeed, of grandmotherhood, for Louise had just given birth to her first daughter, the future Lady Alexandra Duff. This second appearance in a court of law was really beyond all limits. And that pompous ass Willy had written unctuously to the Queen proclaiming his disgust that an honorary colonel in the Prussian Hussars should have become involved in a card-sharping affair.

As after the Mordaunt case, Alexandra's final option was to pack up her bags and take the children to Denmark. From thence she intended to visit Russia. She was away on Edward's fiftieth birthday, which he celebrated in morose isolation. So far as he knew, Alexandra meant to stay away indefinitely, but a near disaster again brought her rushing home. Georgie had contracted the dreaded typhoid. Alexandra, travelling day and night for a week, arrived to find her son out of danger. All was forgiven although not forgotten, and the family reunion was made the happier by the engagement of Princess May of Teck to the Duke of Clarence.

A large house party assembled at Sandringham in the New Year of 1892, but Clarence, whose frail constitution had been undermined by pursuits beyond his strength and whose lack of mental staying-power had perplexed his tutors, succumbed to the widespread influenza epidemic. "We are broken-hearted," the Prince wrote to his mother. Alexandra seemed "turned into marble". Eddy, her great pride, her favourite child, was no more. The Queen overruled her wish to immure him at Sandringham, and to Windsor he was borne.

"Poor me," moaned Victoria, "in my old age to see this promising young life cut short. . . . Poor darling Alix looks a picture of grief and misery." After the funeral she thought Alexandra looked "lovelier than ever in her deep mourning and a long black veil, with a band, on her head".

Blackness and mourning were much to the Queen's taste. Alexandra wrote to her parents, who were celebrating their golden wedding, "I have buried my angel today and with him my happiness." To Lady Granby, who had just lost a son, the Princess wrote, "Pray God these dear ones may have links to draw us up to Him and Eternal Life." For eighteen months she severed herself from Society. Eddy's room was always preserved entirely as it had been at his death. She also mourned the handsome Oliver Montagu, who died soon after her son.

Unhappy indeed were the closing years of Victoria's reign. Weddings there were—George wed to Mary, and more grandchildren and godchildren for Alexandra to dote upon; but there were other funerals too, more clashes with Willy and anxieties about Greece. By 1893 the Greek monarch was bald, depressed and tyrannous, refusing to discuss state affairs with his sons and reducing Olga to tears. Alexandra, who often saw the mote in other people's eyes and not the beam in her own, could not understand why her brother never would allow his children to grow up; in this if in nothing else she almost exactly resembled him. Alexander III died in 1894, and the Princess of Wales spent two months with her bereft sister.

"Alix has been the greatest possible comfort to Minnie," wrote Edward, "and I really don't know what she would have done without her."

At any rate, the new Emperor Nicholas II was kind to his mother and as devoted as was the Kaiser to Queen Victoria, whom the Czar visited in 1896 in the valiant uniform of the Scots Greys. But two parties were growing up in Russia, pro-German headed by the Czar's wife 'Alicky' and pro-British under the Dowager Empress. Between these two masterful women Nicholas danced a faltering minuet, and the path was unconsciously paved for the fatal theocracy of Rasputin with his mixed potions of magic and politics, while the Prince of Wales and the Kaiser exchanged mutual abuse in their efforts to snatch 'Nicky' into an alliance. The wheels of Victorian diplomacy were lightly lubricated with royal macassar. Willy 'dropped the pilot', and Bismarck retreated to his estates after warning Herbert not to stay aboard a ship about to dash itself against the rocks. The Emperor's interference extended to Greece, and Alexandra's dislike of her nephew reached a climax when 'Veelee' became embroiled with Turkey. The Greeks, after improvidently assaulting the Turkish garrisons of Crete against the advice of the powers, invaded Turkish

Macedonia. From both places they were precipitantly removed. The Kaiser, whose sister was married to Crown Prince Constantine, held the Greeks to blame for this ignominy and refused to help. In the midst of the crisis Alexandra implored Queen Victoria:

"Dearest Mama . . . Now the Powers must step in to save them from utter ruin and revolution at Athens . . . No time must be lost."

Marie Mallet found her in 'an awful stew' about Greece. Wilhelm, who had piqued the British government by his famous telegram of congratulation to the Boer President Kruger, cared as little for the Danish monarchy and its Greek offshoot as for his British relations, and with calculated rudeness telegraphed a terse reply to Victoria *en clair*. Alexandra unburdened herself at Sandringham to the German Foreign Secretary and future Chancellor, Von Bulow, a childhood acquaintance at Rumpenheim. The Kruger telegram, she said, showed that the Emperor was 'inwardly our enemy, even if he surpasses himself every time he meets us, in flatteries, compliments and assurances of love and affection. His heartless treatment of his dying father and his behaviour to his mother show that he has as little heart as he has political commonsense'.

This unpleasantness was preceded by the death of Queen Louise of Denmark. Stone deaf, she spent her last years in a wheelchair. "No words can describe our sorrow," wrote Alexandra. The news arrived while she was nursing her husband aboard the *Osborne* at Cowes after the unfortunate banister incident at Waddesdon. Old King Christian retired to Bernstorff, where after Louise died Alexandra and Dagmar stayed with him in turn; when they left he invariably broke down and wept. But there were compensations. The future Edward VIII had become an industrious little companion for 'dear Grannie', hiding behind her skirts when they went to see the big dogs at Sandringham kennels, and creating "a mat for mother with a union jack on it" under Grannie's admiring direction. Daughter Maud had married her sailor cousin, the future Haakon of Norway. They spent their honeymoon at Sandringham: where else, but under Darling Motherdear's tender eye?

The Queen was fading, and the vast theatre which she had stamped with her personality since the death of William IV was shrouded in a crepuscular haze. In the wings the supers and the stagehands of the Marlborough House Set were preparing the flats and the sliders against the exalted moment when a king should reign again. From the year of the Diamond Jubilee the Queen had lived more and more in the past and had relied more and more upon Alexandra. She even deferred to her daughter-in-law in the matter of dress on the great occasion itself, agreeing to relieve the monotony of mourning weeds with gold embroidery on the front of her gown. The Princess of Wales, very much in favour, alone accompanied the Queen on the ceremonial procession to St. Paul's. A movie, one of the first ever exhibited, shows the Queen and Alexandra sitting face to face in the open carriage while surpliced choirs and uniformed bandsmen form a phalanx up the cathedral steps behind them.

The reigning Lord Howe, having maintained the ancestral tradition as Gold Stick, was improbably clad in armour and in this ferrous condition had the misfortune to be thrown by his horse. He landed with a crash beside the state carriage, nearly knocking himself unconscious. Alexandra stood up and urged him into one of the other carriages. He resolutely refused to add incongruity to injury. The battered visor conveyed even more than the muffled curses issuing from within as, remounting, he rode grimly after his Sovereign lady to the end. The Jubilee enabled Alexandra, with the aid of the nation's grocer and leading yachtsman, Sir Thomas Lipton, to organize dinners for the deserving poor of the metropolis. Under her patronage 400,000 people consumed 700 tons of foods at halls all over London. With Lipton's help she also founded the Alexandra Trust to provide the hungry with cheap portions of hot food. The celebrations lasted a fortnight, but the brilliance was overcast: the Duchess of Teck died at Richmond. Mary Adelaide, with her double chins and her gift for friendship, stood next to Alexandra—if awe of the Queen be excepted—in royal popularity.

"Can it be possible," she once said, "that when I go to Heaven I shall meet that murderer Henry VIII? Never! I cannot believe it! Such a bad character!"

After the Jubilee the Queen quietly disappeared behind the arras. Her last Continental progress was to Nice in the spring of 1899 when the whole Royal Family descended *en masse*, to the distaste of Marie Mallet. The place was "literally crawling with

9

Royalties", among them Alexandra and her daughters, who looked "very seedy", especially Maud, who had dyed her hair canary yellow, making her look "quite improper and more like a little milliner than ever". Alexandra's restlessness she found alarming—travel, travel, travel. "I hear," wrote Marie, "that she dreads the possibility of reigning."

The Boer War broke out and Willy arrived puffing with advice for his uncle. In England's hour of embarrassment the Kaiser was ever alert to be of disservice, but on this occasion he was affability personified and even Alexandra was deceived. A pale-blue hunting suit set off the Imperial figure to perfection, and he made a dashing spectacle in a Tyrolean hat bedecked with black cock's feathers. Followed by four jaegers with horns and loaded guns, he set off briskly after the ubiquitous pheasant at Sandringham, triumphing over the disability of the withered arm to perform dexterous feats of one-handed guncraft until the Imperial bag overflowed with little plumed corpses.

The Princess of Wales founded a famous nursing service and soon realized what Florence Nightingale had had to put up with. Her plan to equip a hospital ship for South Africa brought her into conflict with the authorities. When she had beaten the War Office she upset the crew, to whom she appeared domineering, tending to act as captain, head surgeon, matron, purser and deck hand combined. But in one matter she bowed to maritime tradition: the master would conduct religious services aboard and her decision to appoint a ship's chaplain was gracefully withdrawn. Alexandra also pioneered a scheme to provide portable houses for dockers who were dispatched to Capetown to unload stores for the Army. When she found that the cheapest units could be bought in Germany she drew the line. Nothing would induce her to get them from that hated country.

In April 1900 the Prince and Princess of Wales embarked for Copenhagen, travelling via Belgium. While they waited in the train at Brussels station a 15-year-old Belgian student named Sipido, a fanatical anarchist, poked a revolver through the carriage window and fired pointblank at the royal travellers. The bullet whistled through Charlotte Knollys's bun and pierced the upholstery. "No harm done," Edward laconically reported. Alexandra scarcely moved a muscle. "The Princess is none the worse," Edward reassured his friends, "and bore everything with the greatest courage and fortitude." Sipido was eventually freed under police supervision until he came of age. Edward slipped the bullet into an envelope, on which he wrote: "Sipido's bullet, Brussels, April 1900," and consigned it to the archives at Windsor. Had Georgie had his way Sipido would have been "exterminated like a wasp".

Queen Victoria died at Osborne in the evening of 22nd January 1901. Once again Willy "bossed the show". While Edward knelt by his mother's deathbed the Kaiser held her in his arms. With Edward out of the way in London for the proclamation Willy took command of the undertakers, himself measured the Queen for her coffin and, when Edward and his brother Connaught returned, helped to lay her in the lead-covered casket. Strangely the sight of her unloved nephew supervising every last detail made little impression on Alexandra. She more than anyone felt the loss of the imperious mother-in-law who, in her way, had been her friend and guide through the long 'sub-reign' at Marlborough House. She wept also for herself. She might be Queen, but there was only one Victoria.

The reign of Edward VII projected the Marlbocracy into the limelight of the twentieth century. Alexandra created a new dimension of queenship. It is doubtful whether she would have imprinted herself more deeply on her times even if the reign had lasted twice as long as, with her limp and her jewelled 'dog-collar', she moved amiably among her people. She and Edward had drifted apart in the last years of Victoria's reign, but the throne drew them together, and when Edward died in 1910 she grieved like a young girl who had lost her lover.

The dead king was dressed in his field-marshal's uniform. Alexandra took Austen Chamberlain to see him. "He is so peaceful, so like himself," she said unexpectedly. "He always looked like that when he was sleeping—so like a soldier." In some ways she reproduced the sentiments of her predecessor when, after William IV's death, Adelaide determined to see that full honour was paid to her husband's memory. Esher and others tried to compose a message to the Dominions, but the Queen's effort came "straight from her woman's heart" and made Esher's poor attempt "look most forlorn". She wrote: "From the depths of my poor broken heart I wish to express to the whole nation and

our kind people we love so well my deep-felt thanks for their
touching sympathy in my overwhelming sorrow and unspeakable
anguish. Not alone have I lost everything in him, my beloved
husband, but the nation, too, has suffered an irreparable loss."

Her tenderness betrayed "all the love in her soul", thought
Esher; and in a way she seemed happy—the "womanly happiness
of complete possession of the man who was the love of her youth
and, as I fervently believe, of all her life". Once she broke down
crying, "What is to become of me?" and after he had left her she
sat down at a little chair beside the dead king.

"Round the room were all the things just as he had last used
them, with his hats hanging on the pegs as he loved them to do."

Nine monarchs, including Wilhelm, came from Europe for the
funeral; and Margot Asquith could scarcely repress a shudder
when she thought what the terrifying result of a bomb tossed from
Big Ben would have been on the glittering assemblage; she
"blessed this country for its freedom". At Windsor, when the
coffin was lowered and slowly disappeared into the ground,
Alexandra knelt suddenly and covered her face with both hands.

9

Sorrows of Old Age

THE QUEEN MOTHER—"lovely in her widow's weeds"—retired to Sandringham with a taxed income of £70,000, taking Edward's dog Caesar, who had followed the *cortège* behind his master's horse. "Isn't it curious?" she said. "As long as the King lived Caesar never cared for me. . . . Since the King's death he will be with nobody but me." Someone asked her whether she would be styled queen dowager or queen mother. Only the term queen mother, she said, would have any meaning for her. The new Queen Mary told David when he sought information, "I believe the right way to write to me is The Queen & to Grannie Queen Alexandra as she is now the Queen Mother & I am the wife of the King."

For a time Alexandra was inconsolable. "My life is finished, there is nothing left for me in the future, all my things to move, and no garden like there is here"—she meant Buckingham Palace. There followed the long painful removal of her 'things' from the palace back to Marlborough House. Life had suddenly lost its savour. She was not permitted to attend George V's coronation. Shutting herself up at Sandringham, she whispered the coronation prayers in the little church, attended by Princess Victoria and the faithful Probyn and Knollys. But presently she sloughed her depression and reflected on the future. With her mother-in-law's example before her, she shed her weeds and, like Edward, decided to "work to the end". All King Christian's children assembled in Copenhagen in the autumn of 1911 for the last time. Alexandra found 'Veelee' as bald as an egg, worried and petulant; King Frederick prematurely aged; Dagmar groaning with gout. She

herself, short-breathed from bronchitis, wheezed caveats about
the possibility of a 'conflagration' in Europe. The next two years
brought more tragedies. The Duke of Fife, having survived with
his wife and children the shipwreck of the *Delhi* off the African
coast, succumbed to fever in Egypt; King Frederick dropped
dead in a Hamburg street; and 'Veelee' was assassinated by a
lunatic in Salonika. "All is pitchy black again," moaned one of
Alexandra's ladies. The Queen Mother retired weeping to
Hvidore.

Dagmar was at Marlborough House when the Great War broke
out. The sisters informed visitors, "Didn't we tell you that the
Kaiser was a villain?" They stared across at the huge crowds
jamming the roadway before Buckingham Palace, where George
V stood tearfully "in a silence that could almost be felt while the
last moments of the ultimatum to Germany expired; and when
at length the clock boomed out the hour one deep breath was
drawn by all those thousands like a mighty sigh". Dagmar's
perilous journey back to Russia was interrupted by German
troop movements. She was held, fuming, like a prisoner in her
railway coach, but disdained to make any appeal to 'Kaiser Bill'.
At last she reached Hvidore, where she took up the twin-like
photographs of George V and Nicholas II—"My son, and
Alexandra's George, shake hands now."

"God help us and our dear countries!" wrote Alexandra to her
father's old aide, Colonel Rørdam in Denmark. "May our dearly
beloved native country stay outside the struggle and keep her
neutrality until the last in this unjust war, which we in Denmark
knew since 1864 [the year of the rape of the duchies] would come
one day."

The Queen Mother saw in Belgium's fate a reflection of Denmark's half a century earlier. Through her friendship with
Kitchener she received a special war bulletin daily and destroyed
it after reading it. At the age of 70 she felt she had endured more
than her fair share of suffering when she saw members of her
family lined up on opposing sides. Her younger sister Thyra,
Duchess of Cumberland, was left in Germany; Thyra's son, the
Kaiser's son-in-law, fought with the Germans, as did so many
relations from states previously annexed by Prussia. Her nephew
King Constantine of Greece, married to the Kaiser's sister, lived
under perpetual threat of deposition or worse because he was a

suspect pro-German. Denmark avoided the war, but Danes living in Schleswig-Holstein were obliged to fight for 'the Huns'. Yet her greatest trial was to be separated from Dagmar. She regularly corresponded with 'Minnie'. Kitchener was carrying a letter from Alexandra for Dagmar when the *Hampshire* went down.

From the day the *U22* sank the cruiser off the Orkneys in 1916 the Queen Mother's anxiety about Russia slowly turned to alarm. On 21st July 1918 *Le Matin* and other Paris dailies reported the first rumours that her nephew Nicholas II had been shot. Historians writing with hindsight could note that it was his fate to have inherited 'Hamlet's blood' from his Danish mother. He was ruled by his Czarina, who called him 'darling boysy' and herself was branded by the Russian people as 'the German woman' or *nemka*. Blame was visited upon 'Alicky' for passing on haemophilia to the Russian heir Alexis. Dagmar, in constant conflict with her daughter-in-law, was to her son's subjects known as 'the old Danish woman'. Even as the shadows gathered, Rasputin murdered, the country in ferment, the army crushed and mutinous, the Czarina could remark, "I have been on the throne twenty-two years. I know Russia. I know how the people love our family. Who would dare to side against us?" And Nicholas echoed to the British ambassador, Sir George Buchanan: "You tell me, my dear ambassador, that I ought to earn my people's trust. But isn't it rather my people who ought to earn my trust?" He fixed his eyes on the ground, smoked silently, and awaited martyrdom. The execution of the Romanovs had been announced several times since the spring of 1918 after their removal to the 'house of special assignment' at Ekaterinburg.

When the Czarist empire crashed beyond all reasonable doubt the problem of offering the Imperial Family asylum perplexed George V and his mother and the British government. The King would have preferred their seeking refuge in Switzerland or Denmark. An attempt to smuggle them out through Murmansk on a British warship was subjected to fatal delays because the Czar's daughters contracted measles and he refused to move without them. Even a lukewarm promise of hospitality by the British government was bitterly opposed by left-wing elements in Britain and venomously vetoed by the Bolsheviks, while Denmark's pleas to free the Czar were brutishly rebuffed. The British Cabinet feared an outbreak of strikes in munitions factories and dockyards. There was also a curious story that Rasputin had leaked information to the Germans which led to the torpedoing of the *Hampshire*. And so eleven people were butchered in the cellar at Ekaterinburg to make a communist empire. The Czar, his ailing wife in her wheelchair, their haemophiliac son and heir, their four daughters and four members of their household were lured into the basement in the early hours of 17th July on the pretext that the White Guards were about to attack. "But for that tragedy," wrote the Prime Minister, David Lloyd George, "this country cannot be in any way held responsible." Early in the Terror the Dowager Empress reluctantly left for Livadia, where she lingered in daily expectation of the family's release. Late in November she wrote to Nicholas: "I get letters from Aunt Alix and Valdemar from time to time, but they are so slow in coming, and I just sit and wait."

Her letter was never answered. For a long time she refused to accept the terrible truth. Alexandra collapsed with shock; she was also consumed with anxiety for Dagmar. There was still no news of her sister when in December 1918 Douglas Haig made his triumphal entry into London. Her intention was to meet the victorious field-marshal in The Mall and congratulate him, but a messenger brought her a discreet caveat from the palace explaining that such an interruption might hazard police control of the crowds. No reply was sent, and the King assumed that his mother, with Lady Haig and her schoolgirl daughters, would be content to watch the procession from the windows of Marlborough House. Not so. They appeared innocently at the windows with little Union flags, but as the procession approached Alexandra suddenly rose with the familiar "I go!" and, tapping her way through the crowd followed by the Haigs, gained the open avenue. The coach with its red-liveried flunkeys bore down. Alexandra stepped into the road and held up her cane. The procession halted. Haig stood up and she took his hand, over which he bowed as the cheers crashed around them. The police had no trouble.

Five months passed before Dagmar could be rescued from her precarious refuge on the Black Sea. The King sent the battleship *Marlborough*, but the Dowager ex-Empress refused to step aboard without her imperilled friends, including Helen, Duchess of Mecklenburg; and Princess Yousoupoff, mother of Dagmar's grandson-in-law, Prince Felix, who had plotted against Rasputin. There was good cause for Dagmar's fears. The murdered victims of the revolutionaries were tossed daily into the sea from Yalta pier with stones tied to their feet. One survivor went off his head, having seen in the murky depths the corpses of hundreds of priests, nuns, nurses and Czarist officers in uniform floating upright, arms and clothes waving in the current as though they were alive.

The two aged sisters were reunited at Marlborough House. Dagmar's plight was parlous. Accustomed to great wealth, now she was penniless and bereft. A woman less obdurate would have crumpled before these disasters, but she settled at Hvidore on an allowance from Alexandra.

At home Alexandra concentrated on her charities with almost limitless generosity, on the scale of Adelaide. She founded Alexandra Day, still a British institution under the great-grand-daughter who bears her name, and annually drove through London's decorated streets. The sale of flowers trebled when she showed herself. But Rose Day became 'horrible' to her. She began to dread the inexorable pilgrimage. "I am getting too old and stupid for those pleasures," she wrote. Begging letters flowed into Marlborough House, deserving cases mixed up with rogues and vagabonds. She could refuse nobody, and Probyn and Knollys, who cosseted her like faithful spaniels, brooded over her depleted funds. One villain had a letter smuggled out of prison to her. Miss Knollys tried to dissuade her. "*Basta!* Give him ten pounds," was the reply. "He will need it when he comes out."

In her last years she wore a startling auburn wig which tended to slip to one side. "Is it straight?" she would ask those around her. Queen Marie of Rumania remembered: "To the end there was about Aunt Alix something invincible, something exquisite and flower-like. Her way of coming into a room was incomparable, her smile of welcome lit everything up. She gave you the same joy as a beautiful rose or an absolutely faultless carnation. . . ."

On one wrist she wore a gold bracelet in the shape of a snake with a jewelled head; so much was it part of Alexandra that it seemed to have "grown on her arm". Aged servants tottered around her in the garments of another age. They lived with the Queen Mother in an aura of faded glories, shadows of a world from which they would gladly have departed with her to another sphere.

"Ugly old woman," she said, staring into the looking-glass. "Nobody likes me any more."

Journeys to Hvidore became no longer possible or prudent. London was too much for her. At Sandringham she found not only peace and quiet but also economy dictated by her lavish outlay on charities. There it did not matter how unpunctual she was, or whether she was so deaf that she could no longer play the piano with pleasure. She could be as dilatory and as vague as she pleased. How nice to be late for everything! The clocks, which Edward had had advanced half an hour in the vain hope of making her keep time, held no terror for her now. The simple life suited her, with drives around the Sandringham estate patting the heads of tenants' children and holding the hands of the dying. Except for family reunions she rarely appeared at Marlborough House, but she attended the wedding of the later 'Bertie', the future George VI, to Elizabeth of Glamis. She was among the first to know that Britain would probably have another queen regnant: the future Elizabeth II was born five months before Alexandra died. George V had gallantly sacrificed Sandringham to his mother, although his large family could have used it to greater advantage.

"It is full of so many happy memories of my whole married life," wrote Queen Mary to the Prince of Wales, "tho' of course Papa & I went thro' sad times—especially when poor Grannie became so frail those last two years."

On 1st December 1924 the old Queen celebrated her eightieth birthday, her last, when she was complaining that "my old head is coming to a breakdown soon". She sliced her birthday cake in the Sandringham ballroom and sat through two films: *Monsieur Beaucaire* and a series of news reels taken of her. In the same year she lost the incomparable Probyn, then over 90, who had served her to the end. Lord Knollys also died after having served Edward as private secretary for forty years. The only survivor of the Edwardian Court was Charlotte Knollys, who ailed and fretted.

Early in 1925 Alexandra wrote to the King: "I feel *completely* collapsed—I shall soon go." In her 'weariness of spirit' she sighed for death. Queen Mary found her decay unbearably poignant—

"It is so hard to see that beautiful woman come to this"; for Alexandra had been compared to Rider Haggard's 'She', the incredible old woman with the beauty of a young girl. Now she could understand no one and no one could understand 'Darling Motherdear' any more. On 20th November, after a heart attack, she died peacefully at Sandringham in the presence of her family, and Queen Mary kissed her forehead and her cheek. David appeared at the deathbed with two toy dogs for his grandmother, but he was too late. Her body was taken to Westminster a week later—the wails of Charlotte Knollys ululated in the still air of Sandringham—and a gun carriage bore her to Windsor among the fainting snowflakes.

"Now darling Mama lies near dear Eddy," wrote Queen Mary, recalling her first lost love nearly forty years before.

After Alexandra's death a bunch of the first snowdrops found in the park at Sandringham was for years dutifully placed on her memorial in the church of St. Mary Magdalene there. Thousands of her son's subjects at home and abroad, from highest to lowliest, contributed more than £200,000 to honour her memory. The money was spent on the development of district nursing, on the provision of pensions for Queen's Nurses, and the balance on the statuary group which is to be seen in the wall of Marlborough House opposite St. James's Palace. In 1946 her jewels were sold at Christie's. They realized £100,000.

Queen Mary

10

Early Influences

IN THE WEEK before the birth of Queen Mary at Kensington Palace on a Sunday in May 1867 a Mr. Mill rose in the Commons to propose that votes for women, disarmingly described as 'persons', should be incorporated in the Reform Bill, the first since the turbulence of 1832. The motion was lost, *Punch* observing cynically that "several enthusiastic Mamas", in commemoration of that bold feminist speech, had christened their daughters Amelia, Emily or Millicent because any of those names could be abbreviated into Milly. Such was the humour of the day. But it signally failed to impress Prince Francis, Duke of Teck, as His Serene Highness anxiously awaited news of his overweight but amiable Mary Adelaide, who was with child.

"Let us hope," he had written to his sister in Germany, "that a nice baby will be born there in the lovely month of May."

Unhappily, it turned out to be one of the coldest Mays on record, and a gentleman complained to *The Times* about it. The Duke's hopes were realized soon after midnight on 26th May. But John Stuart Mill might never have existed. After family consultations, inevitably overshadowed by Queen Victoria, the child was baptized Victoria Mary Augusta Louise Olga Pauline Claudine Agnes. Originally Victoria was to have been her third name, after her mother's and her aunt's, the fabulous 'Aunt Augusta' of this narrative, but the Queen prevailed and Victoria took the lead. The child was called Mary, the name which the Crusaders had popularized after their return from the Holy Land. The family shortened it to May, after the month of her birth; to Mary Adelaide she was her "little mayflower" and her beloved first "chick". The Queen, then in the fourth year of widowhood, marvelled at the strange accident that had brought her little relation into the world two days before her own birthday and in the very bedroom at Kensington Palace where she had been born forty-six years earlier.

An even more curious accident was Mary's rise from poor kinswoman of the British Royal Family to the position of first lady, for on her father's side, alas, there was much to be regretted. There lived in an undistinguished villa in Vienna an old gentleman whose prospects of inheriting the kingdom of Würrtemburg had been ruined by his marriage to a commoner in 1835. Francis of Teck was a product of this morganatic union. Mary thus inherited the mixed blood of her grandfather and of the beautiful Hungarian *ingénue*, Claudine, Countess Rhèdey of Kis-Redé. Through this lady Mary claimed direct descent from the House of Aba to which the rough Continental empires of Europe had paid homage ten centuries ago. But the ruling King of Würrtemberg, stiff with pride and trivially embroiled in feuds about protocol, precedence and patronage, considered he had overstepped the bounds of royal decency and duty when he conferred upon her the title Countess of Hohenstein. This was a scintillating guerdon of favour by the head of a kingdom fortunate to have survived the ravages of Napoleon's frequent excursions; but Würrtemberg controlled the head waters of the Danube, and there was a good deal to be said for that.

In three years the countess produced three children, Claudine, Franz (in the year of Victoria's Accession) and Amélie, but in three more years she was tragically removed. One day in 1841 her horse threw her at a review of Austrian troops near Vienna, and she was trampled to death beneath the hooves of a squadron of galloping cavalry. Sixty years later Mary, then Princess of Wales, dedicated a tablet to her grandmother's memory in the wayside church at Erdó Szent-György in the Transylvanian mountains, where she was buried. Duke Alexander never remarried. He endured into old age, a Falstaffian figure with grand moustaches stained by the nicotine of black cheroots. Grosspapa, smelling strongly of tobacco, lived in impecunious isolation with his memories and his antique weapons of war and other relics of a military career. Most of these treasures and all his furniture were sold to pay his debts.

Mary's maternal grandfather was Adolphus Frederick, the seventh, youngest and most dutiful of George III's sons. He will be recalled as that Duke of Cambridge who arranged William's marriage to Adelaide. In another matter of the heart he had been conspicuously unsuccessful, having helped to foist the unfortunate Caroline of Brunswick upon his eldest brother. A soldier by choice, although Caroline thought he looked like a sergeant "and so vulgar with his ears full of powder", he became Viceroy of Hanover. His own choice of a bride during the celebrated 'race for an heir' after Princess Charlotte's death fell upon Augusta, the youngest daughter of the Landgrave of Hesse-Cassel, a great-granddaughter of George II. Their children were George, who succeeded him as Duke of Cambridge and commanded the British Army for thirty-nine years, 'Aunt Augusta' and, finally, in 1833, Mary Adelaide. The pre-emptive primogeniture of his brothers Kent and Cumberland deprived Adolphus at almost one stroke of the thrones of England and Hanover. But he was happy to be closely allied in blood "to two great and happy families that are governing two happy and prosperous countries". Until Victoria's birth the Cambridges were high in the succession. Adolphus Frederick became deaf and eccentric. In church he invariably replied "By all means" when the parson intoned "Let us pray"; and at the words "For we brought nothing into the world, neither may we carry anything out", he would abruptly interject: "True, true . . . too many calls upon us for that." Usually he trebled his phrases—'the triptology', Horace Walpole called this peculiarity of the Hanoverians. "Mustn't steal, mustn't steal, mustn't steal," he would mutter when the chaplain enumerated the Commandments. Apart from consorting with musicians, he upset Victoria's decorum by some light raillery at the expense of The Beloved One at a public dinner. The deafer he grew the more he shouted, assuming that everyone else was deaf.

"The Cambridges are gone and the castle is as still as the grave," they said when he left Windsor.

Eventually the Queen and Albert came to admire his sterling qualities, not the least of which was a unique ability in any son of George III to live within his income. He died in 1850.

The widowed Augusta lived on to the age of 91. The English language came to her with great difficulty, and to the end of her days she spoke with a pronounced German accent. She and her

10

daughter Mary Adelaide sailed like galleons between Kew Cottage and London—"the stout parties from Kew", in Clarendon's mordant phrase. In old age the Duchess covered her pomatumed locks with a splendid cap and to her young granddaughter Mary she was an awesome, heavy-browed but kindly figure who adhered grimly to the customs and fashions of the eighteenth century. At St. James's Palace, her abode from 1875, she kept a cap and wig on a bedside stand and when visitors arrived she would clap it on so that it perched slightly athwart her head, like Alexandra's wig. Old age bent her down. Tosti, the operatic singer, recalled kneeling on the floor to look into her face. She died at St. James's Palace in 1889.

Wealth distinguished the Cambridges from most of their relations. Rich by any standard, they enjoyed all the prerogatives conferred by cash, land and investment; that is, they could afford to be parsimonious or generous as the fancy seized them. George, the son, lived in style. As a grandson of George III he was a privileged and accepted disciple at the Courts of King William and Queen Victoria; and we may recall how he carried tales of Windsor to his marvelling younger cousins at Rumpenheim. Once when he almost succumbed to scarlet fever in Hanover his father forced a glass of Steinberger into him, at which he revived. Steinberger was always served on his birthday after that to commemorate the miraculous recovery. He grew into a gay and heroic figure who would have adorned a throne as elegantly as he sat a horse. Those accidents of birth already noted robbed England of a monarch who might have reigned even longer than Victoria; but George, feeling himself free after the succession had been secured by his cousins, indulged those amorous fancies for which his 'wicked uncles' had been notorious. He committed the unpardonable crime of marrying for love outside the royal circle. His roving blue eye settled upon Louisa Fairbrother, an actress; but he was bolder than his Uncle William and in 1847 he actually married her. Together they produced a little crop of three male FitzGeorges, George, Adolphus and Augustus. The Duke copied Uncle William's practice of naming his progeny after the sons of George III. They all settled snugly in Queen Street, Mayfair, with two other older children brought by Louisa to the common hearth, stepsister Louisa Katherine and stepbrother Charles Manners Sutton.

The Queen was shocked. Never would she acknowledge Mrs. FitzGeorge, who is ominously omitted from her diaries. Over the years George Cambridge paid out more than £100,000 to maintain his sons in solvency. Family commitments and genuine devotion to Louisa failed to deter him from solacing himself for thirty-five years with one of his earlier loves, Mrs. Beauclerk, and when she died in 1881 he "cried dreadfully". Another bitter blow fell when his son, George FitzGeorge, left the Army to become —as another family friend, Lady Geraldine Somerset, vehemently expostulated—"a writer in the Press!!!! the most horrible occupation a man can possibly take to".

During his long régime as generalissimo of the Army he reconstituted the Staff College at Camberley. This 'Royal George', too, was a 'triptologist' and deaf like his father. His "What, what, what?" and his "Who, who, who?" exploded like grenades thrown in clusters of three; Wellington in old age was much like him. George was the first member of the Royal Family to "make a practical trial of the motor-car in the early stages of its legal existence". In old age his memory was phenomenal: he could still recite the whole of "John Gilpin" without a pause. He remained attached to Louisa to the end and was buried beside her in a vault at Kensal Rise. 'Uncle George' was one of those eccentrics who helped to shape and flavour the early life of the future Queen Mary, who wept "floods" at his death. His equestrian statue lingers behind Haig's in Whitehall near Horse Guards, his spiritual home.

Two others, equally formidable, stand out like beacons along Mary's high road to the throne. They were George's two sisters. The elder, Augusta, we have already encountered; she became Grand Duchess of Mecklenburg-Strelitz and survived into the 'terrible' twentieth century as the only living expert on the coronation and Court etiquette of William IV and Adelaide. After her marriage to 'Uncle Fritz', the Grand Duke, she settled at Strelitz Schloss in north-east Germany, 8 miles from Mirow, the birth-place of Queen Charlotte, where Mary and her brothers often played beneath a great beech tree which had cast its shade over the old Queen as a child. Little ever escaped the sparrow eye of Aunt Augusta when she visited London. She was a woman of violent prejudice. Her *bête noire* was Mr. Gladstone, whom she denounced as a "wicked madman", as far to the Left as she was to the Right. Throughout her life she fervently believed in the Divine Right and in the sacred mission of the Royal Family, herself included. A footman once had the temerity to describe the equestrian statue of George III, her venerated grandfather, as "the old gentleman on the copper hoss"; she nearly swooned. When she discovered that the future George V was reading Greville's memoirs to her niece Mary she warned them to break the habit—it was "full of lies".

Another pet aversion was the Consort. She and her sister Mary Adelaide to the end of their lives held George III in almost reverential awe, but Albert's German 'correctness' had reduced their proud style of "Princesses of Great Britain and Ireland" to "Princesses of Cambridge". Augusta never forgot, never forgave, and never accepted the insult. But the gaiety of the Cambridge family conflicted with the prim ideals of Victoria and Albert; apart from anything else, they never forgave George's regrettable lapse into an irregular marriage.

Augusta had been present at Mary's birth and, when Mary Adelaide died, became her chief confidante and adviser. Torrents of prose were poured out. When Mary became engaged to the Duke of Clarence she was so "flabbergasted" that she nearly tottered to the floor. "God grant that he may become worthy of her!" she wrote to her sister, and hoped the news would not un-hinge Franz's already creaking mind. When Mary became engaged to George she flew to her from Strelitz. Her meanness in money matters was reflected by her refusal to provide rubber tyres for her carriage wheels, yet when Mary married she and 'Uncle Fritz' contributed £1,000 towards the trousseau, despite their feelings that marriage to her dead fiancé's brother was unseemly. George Cambridge considered this union "unfeeling and hor-rible"; the same could have been said of his own to a printer's daughter who displayed her person on the London stage. Augusta overcame her misgivings, and when Edward was born in 1894 the very thought of being the great-aunt of a future King of England made her head reel and she wept with joy and embraced everyone within reach.

On the death of Mary Adelaide in 1898 Mary—"an angel of mercy"—joined her aunt in the South of France. Augusta had need of her, for apart from her sister's death she had another cross to bear: her 19-year-old granddaughter Marie was *enceinte*, having been seduced by a footman at the family *schloss*. Marie was not so much the victim of Hecht, the footman, as of the feudal system prevalent at the castle. Hecht had orders to light the princess to her virginal bedroom every night, a procedure which so worked upon his genes that he felt compelled to explain to her the mysteries of sex, a word which caused a shudder then and, for different reasons, causes a shudder even now. The scandal was hushed up. Hecht was dismissed for 'theft', no doubt rightly, for if the larceny of a young woman's reputation in such circumstances is not theft it is difficult to know what is; in earlier times he would have been hoist for treason. The outraged father, Augusta's only son, banished Marie from his sight and forbade her name ever to be mentioned in his presence. When Hecht resorted to blackmail all was indeed 'pitchy black'. But there was much sympathy for Marie at Windsor. The Queen felt sure she had been drugged; the future George V was equally convinced that she had been hypnotized. However that may be, Mary took the royal transgressor under her wing, patched up a peace between Marie and her parents, drove openly with her on the promenade at Nice, and ultimately she was married off to an obliging French count twenty years her senior. The marriage was dissolved ten years later and Marie made a second and less embarrassing venture into matrimony.

The onset of the twentieth century was an affront to Augusta, but she told her niece: "My old loving heart will be with you in the ensuing century as it is and has ever been in this." However, she thoroughly disliked the new trends, all those telephones, electric lights, motor-cars, the cinema and women smoking. An additional cause of annoyance was Count Zeppelin, a neighbour, who had begun to construct his ridiculous airship almost in her backyard. Augusta felt sick at heart; one might see "even Sovereigns flying up into the air". Nothing but ill could come of the new century: she was grieved but not surprised when her husband, prematurely aged and blind, died at Strelitz in 1904. She was in England at the time, it being her fate never to be at hand when her mother, her husband and other relations breathed their last. Once again Mary was her rock of strength.

"She will indeed be a Queen," wrote Augusta when Mary ascended the throne. There followed an intimate correspondence on how the new queen consort should be named. Her first name, it will be recollected, was Victoria, but she could not possibly be called Queen Victoria, and all her life she had been known as May. She could hardly sign herself Victoria Mary, her husband having rooted objections to 'double names'; and in the end King George approved the name by which she is known to history. The Queen, who seems to have had little say in the matter, thought it 'curious' to be rechristened at the age of 43.

Queen Mary found the early weeks of the reign particularly exasperating. Her mother-in-law, inspired by Sister Dagmar, quibbled about questions of precedence. Aunt Augusta, who was suffering from a gumboil, was furious with 'Minnie', and her quill squeaked savagely: "May that pernicious influence soon depart!" But the vexations at last melted away, and the bestowal of the Garter on Augusta's son, the Grand Duke, made the old lady "hop" with pleasure. She was then 88, too frail to travel to London for her niece's coronation by any means, ancient or modern, an 'aerobike' being out of the question. But there were compensations. The citizens of Strelitz regarded their august chatelaine as the greatest living authority on coronations, as she had attended those of William IV and Adelaide, Queen Victoria and Edward VII and Alexandra, and they invaded her *schloss* with songs and bouquets and strewed her path with blossoms. She felt quite like a queen herself, but where Augusta radiated joy over the coronation of 1911 the Queen Mother put a damper on the celebrations by repeating loudly in Mary's presence: "Eddy should be King, not Georgie."

Although Mary had been born in the week of Mr. Mill's famous speech on the rights of women, she grew up with little sympathy for the suffragettes who plagued her early years on the throne. When Miss Emily Wilding Davison flung herself under the King's horse at the 1913 Derby the Queen was more concerned for the "poor jockey" Jones, who had been thrown, than for dead Emily. Her aunt vigorously agreed.

"Can these females not be shut up on some Island?" inquired Augusta.

From then until her death the Dowager Grand Duchess followed her niece's activities with undiminished pleasure and interest. In her last years she suffered from sciatica and used a ear trumpet. In 1912, when Mary visited her after her ninetieth birthday, she found her dressed in black with a black bonnet trimmed with a spray of white feathers and fastened with velvet ribbons under the chin. To everyone's astonishment she ventured forth for the first time in one of the new horseless carriages, returning impressed but with a back ache, which she attributed entirely to the twentieth century. Aunt and niece met for the last time during a state visit to Berlin in 1913, when the old lady was shown movies of their embracing. "Fancy our going *kissing* all over the world!" she marvelled. Later when the King and Queen visited France she thought it "not nice" that Mary should have to ride in a state carriage with a *President*'s wife. It was *lèse majesté*, no less. The outbreak of the Great War shocked Augusta profoundly—"my country at war with the country of my adoption!" From her wheelchair she directed inquiries through the Crown Princess of Sweden, a daughter of Edward VII's brother Connaught, about her numerous relations who were fighting on either side, and managed to maintain a correspondence with Queen Mary to the end.

"Tell the King," she wrote, "that it is a stout old English heart that is ceasing to beat."

That was her last message before she died, uttering the one word "May!" The Queen received the news in December 1916 during the political crisis which brought down the Asquith Government and elevated David Lloyd George to power. The old autocrat, assuming the role of second mother to her niece, had exerted a powerful influence on Mary. Above all she showed her the best in two disparate ways of life, the English and the German, and it was the Grand Duchess's fierce patriotism that kindled in the Queen a love of Britain and the British that glowed to the end.

The other remarkable woman in Mary's life was her mother. It was Mary's destiny to suffer from the unpredictability not only of her mother-in-law but also of Mary Adelaide. Her mother was late in keeping appointments, later still in paying her bills, but earlier in doing a kindness than most people who kept good time. Where she was stout and hearty, a jovial Gargamelle, Alexandra was slim and elegant. Yet had there existed modern techniques of public opinion sampling these two princesses would no doubt have shared the top place in any royal popularity poll. 'Fat Mary' endeared herself to the London crowds as she drove to St. James's in one of her numerous unpaid conveyances, which groaned under her weight, especially when she threw her substantial arms about as though to crush the whole population of the Great Wen in a loving embrace. Such exercises were frowned upon at Windsor; they were out of harmony with the Queen's sombre mood.

Mary Adelaide remained beautiful, with deep blue eyes, natural platinum hair and delicate fair skin, even after time had equipped her with rather more than one chin. The truth is that she was a compulsive *gourmand*. She consumed large quantities of hot buttered toast as *entremêts*, licking her fingers with enjoyment. Love of unsuitable foods had been transmitted to her through her German ancestry, although she was but a shadow compared with the old Queen of Würrtemberg noted earlier in these pages. Her ballooning *embonpoint* was a barrier to romance, and the family efforts to marry her off to some muscular and capable prince usually ended with Mary Adelaide in tears and the hasty retirement of one suitor after another. She had almost surrendered hope when Prince Franz of Teck, sedulously coaxed by the Prince of Wales, appeared on the scene. Franz was four years her junior, and when he offered his heart to Mary Adelaide among the rhododendrons in Kew Gardens she accepted him with bounding alacrity. In such circumstances it was not prudent to scan too closely his Hungarian antecedents. After his mother's tragic death Franz, stalwart and debonair, became the protégé of Franz Josef. The military bearing, the soft and appealing eyes, the waxed moustaches, the imperial beard, assured him a favoured position at the Viennese Court. In the year of Alexandra's marriage to Edward he had been created a Serene Highness (because of the tainted blood he could never be royal) and entitled Prince of Teck.

The wooing of Mary Adelaide proceeded briskly. They were married in June 1866 in the church at Kew in the presence of the Queen, inescapable in her mourning weeds. Victoria thought Franz had been dragged into marriage by those incorrigible match-makers, the Cambridges. But she was not displeased, although her practical interest in obstetrics caused her a pang when, at the age of 33, Mary Adelaide proudly announced her first pregnancy. Childbirth for a woman of her girth and age was a hazardous proceeding in those days, and the Crown Princess

Frederick in Berlin was thoroughly alarmed. However, the huge enterprise was skilfully managed. Franz wanted "a nice baby" and Mary Adelaide resolutely obliged. The future Queen Mary was safely delivered at Kensington, the Duchesse d'Aumale posted off to tell the Duchess of Cambridge at Kew, and the nation rejoiced. The Queen, so demure and diminutive, when she came to inspect the "little mayflower" found the size of Mary Adelaide "fearful", all very regrettable.

Undaunted, indeed, encouraged, Mary Adelaide went on to present Franz with three sons. Mary was followed by Adolphus (Dolly) in 1868, Francis (Frank) in 1870, and Alexander George in 1874. The last-born had his names contracted to Alge, and on his advent—"another and *still* bigger boy!"—the Queen thought it hardly rational. In one way and another the Teck family outflowed their apartments at Kensington. Besides, they distrusted the pond, from which the baby Mary caught an almost fatal fever at two months old. The Queen cautiously, even reluctantly, placed at their disposal the additional refuge of White Lodge in Richmond Park, where the young Prince of Wales had spent so many agonizing months seeking refreshment for the mind.

At Richmond the Duke of Teck vegetated in pointless pursuits. The sin of the father had been visited upon the son. He had displayed soldierly qualities as an *aide de camp* to the Austrian commander at the battle of Solferino, but his military career was brief and blighted. Defective eyesight permitted him little more than a misty glimpse of the enemy in the Egyptian campaign of 1882. Thereafter he was denied useful employment. Historians have never made it clear whether this decision was the result of his intellectual shortcomings or his deficiency of royal blood. Disraeli, who charmed Mary Adelaide as he charmed the Queen, hoped to send him to Ireland as Viceroy; Gladstone had entertained similar aspirations for the Prince of Wales. But the Queen would have no member of the Royal Family embroiled in Irish politics. So Franz tasted the bitter waters of Mara. Most of his time was spent rearranging the rooms or landscaping the grounds, chopping at rhododendrons, planting roses, or dutifully stepping two paces behind Mary Adelaide as she fluttered, late but radiant, from church bazaar to garden party, from art gallery to exhibition, from drawing room to soirée. This depressing existence burdened his spirits. And there was worse. Franz was by no means the first penniless foreign prince to seek his fortune in England, but his expectations were totally defeated by Mary Adelaide's inexorable extravagance. She tended to disburse money which she did not possess. By multiplying and subtracting, adding or dividing, she evolved a chartered accountant's nightmare.

Tradesmen building up quiet businesses in the purlieus of Richmond and Kingston-on-Thames began by loving her as orders poured into their honoured premises; but as time went on and bills remained unpaid apprehension gave way to consternation and alarm to anger, and they began battering at the door of White Lodge. It had been much the same at Kensington. A Mr. Barker had opened up there with every prospect of modest profit from groceries. Mary Adelaide became his most formidable client. Despite that, he flourished sufficiently to make a large donation to a local church hall, which the Duchess of Teck was prevailed upon to open. Spreading her arms towards him on the platform, Mary Adelaide with one of her most enchanting smiles moved a special vote of thanks to Mr. Barker to whom, as she neatly put it, they all owed so much.

Bountiful in large matters, she economized in small. Like a squirrel she hoarded the most trivial articles of domestic use: old envelopes, unfranked stamps, bits of string and brown paper, defunct lampwicks, snippets of thread, buttons, stumps of sealing-wax and candles. Waste not want not, she would say as she launched out on superb spending sprees, an expensive bonnet for 'Mayflower', or new suits for the male 'chicks', or a subscription to an old people's home. She was the despair of the duns and the delight of the poor. She feverishly nourished her mind with books and turned night into day reading anything which fired her enthusiasm. Sometimes she would rise at cock crow but deprive the family of her presence until the middle of the afternoon because she simply could not put down a book she had started. Or if she did not read in her 'brown den' or her 'blue boudoir' she wrote: volumes of diaries and innumerable letters, dashing them off with gusto whenever she felt she had something to say, which she invariably had. Or she would sit up half the night talking, and weary the whole family with waiting around for their meals the next day. The years at White Lodge were certainly not wasted. Mary Adelaide's inexhaustible works of charity benefited thousands of indigent poor, and her open-handed manner of dispensing monetary relief rivalled that of Queen Alexandra in her later years.

In this atmosphere of restless do-gooding Mary developed into a thoughtful, studious girl. It would be an exaggeration to compare White Lodge with Marlborough House, but Mary Adelaide gathered around her a host of bright stars of literature, art, science, music and the stage, from W. S. Gilbert and Du Maurier to Huxley, Bradlaugh, Millais and Beerbohm Tree. The more ebullient her mother, the more sparkling the company, the more Mary shrank into a shell of self-criticism. Did she really know anything? Mary Adelaide firmly believed in the theory that children should be reared in quiet repose so that their little minds could mature: the young were at best second-class citizens. Had the television existed then it is possible that it would have been switched off until after the children were in bed, and that her irrepressible chatter would then have proved more entertaining than the programmes.

Money dripped off Mary Adelaide's fingers like hot butter. Parliament had provided her with an income of £5,000, to which the Duchess of Cambridge added £2,000, but this was insufficient. The Tecks spent twice their revenue. The situation could not last. Appeals to Queen Victoria for loans were rejected. Exile offered the only alternative to duns and debts. After sixteen years of married life, which the old Duchess had subsidized with £60,000 without reducing the deficit, the establishments at Kensington Palace and White Lodge were closed down, possessions sold to satisfy the more pressing creditors, and the Tecks dispatched to Florence. Such a wrench!

II

Exile and Grief

FLORENCE provided Mary with a solid foundation of culture which was to endure all her life. The Duke of Teck maintained his high serenity in the midst of comparative penury, and Mary Adelaide energetically wooed the celebrities of Dante's city, including the fabulous Princess Woroznoff, who felt naked unless she loaded herself with twelve ropes of matched pearls drooping to her knees, and other women of the Czarist and European patriciate who looked as though they had just burgled Garrard's. Artists flocked to Mary Adelaide's *salon*. Economy was kept at arm's length. Language tutors were engaged for the teenage daughter and for Alge (the other two brothers were continuing their education at home); but while Florence opened Mary's mind it never quite conquered her natural reserve. Where her mother was extrovert Mary was almost *farouche*: she rarely spoke unless spoken to, and Mary Adelaide's tendency to comment on her 'shyness' before strangers was unhelpful. Nor, of course, would Mary become one of the beauties of an age of beautiful women; she self-deprecatingly contrasted her 'plainness', which existed only in her imagination, with that of Queen Charlotte.

For some time the Duke of Teck had complained of a mysterious rattling inside his head; he often clapped his hands over his ears to deaden the noise. It was therefore not surprising that he suffered a cerebral haemorrhage, which disabled the left arm. Yet neither Franz's reduced health nor the volcanic rumblings of the creditor classes impeded Mary Adelaide's intrepid hospitality. While Florentine duns besieged her borrowed villa, 'I Cedri', the prancing royalties of the Continent—the "royal mob" who so perplexed Victoria—banqueted or danced or listened to chamber music within. A discreet period of absence from Italy was indicated, if only for the Duke's peace of mind. The Tecks found a new base at an hotel on Lake Lucerne, where the Duke complained about the accommodation, the food, the service and the swarms of loud German tourists. His serenity was frequently shattered by robust laughter, and he was relieved to exchange the pandemonium of hotel life for the old and pompous formality of the narrow-minded, austere and feud-riddled Court of Würrtemberg.

This interlude lasted five months. It is significant because Mary met one of those *entrepreneurs* who have emerged in almost every generation to bring reluctant princes and shy princesses together. Such a one was Queen Olga of Greece, who happened to be at Gmunden with other *bourgeois* royalties. Olga, a niece of Czar Alexander II, took an instant liking to the unassuming Princess May, whose level temperament so contrasted with the volatile character of her husband and the Christian relations. Nine years later, when the future George V was serving with the Mediterranean Fleet, she talked much of Mary—the Duke of Teck's "dearest Pussycat"—to the young naval officer. "Dear tootsums", she implied, was just made for Mary; it was only three months before their marriage.

The Continental relations could not understand the parsimony of the English relations; naturally, for they had not been called upon to pay Mary Adelaide's bills. But finally the exile ended. Some debts were settled, others deferred or forgotten, and the Queen and the Duchess of Cambridge prepared to welcome the royal Micawbers home. They arrived on May's eighteenth birthday, Mary Adelaide, more immense than ever, being swathed in bandages after a fall which delayed their departure from Florence. Their joy at the homecoming was overshadowed by the death of Duke Alexander, but 'Grosspapa' was soon forgotten in the excitement of Mary's confirmation. She was now equipped to be presented at Court.

It was 1885. The Queen had begun to note Mary's "niceness", the Duchess of Cambridge thought her "very beautiful". These compliments nearly drove the asp-like companion, Geraldine Somerset, out of her mind: she considered Princess May "plain", to say the least. Life in the comfortable Victorian environment of White Lodge resumed its chequered course after the two years of severance, with balls and parties and reunions in Society, interspersed by visits to stately homes, including Luton Hoo. Mostly at other people's expense the Tecks supported an establishment befitting their dignity, with butlers and grooms, footmen in identical liveries, dressers, cooks and nearly a dozen maids, with three coachmen to tend the Teck equipage, including a barouche, a landau, a brougham, a waggonette, a dog-cart and a phaeton. Mary had returned to "our beloved home" as reticent and as withdrawn as ever. But her imagination had broadened and her quest for enlightenment had been quickened. She was provided with a French companion, Hélène Bricka, whose main purpose appeared to be to fill in the hours while they waited for Mary Adelaide to appear at meals. They read history, poetry and philosophy for six hours a day, until Mary felt herself as educated as any young woman of her day, and better than most of her rank. Bricka, who wore a curled wig and spectacles, remained her confidante until her death thirty years later.

At her coming-out Mary was a personable young woman, thoughtful, studious and observant, the antithesis of the Prince of Wales's daughters, the "whispering Wales sisters"; Louise, who to Mary's astonishment was allowed to marry a commoner, the Earl (later Duke) of Fife; Toria, who was prevented from marrying a commoner and never married; and Maud, the future Queen of Norway. At great country houses she met the Gladstones, Disraeli and his wife Mary Anne, Lord Salisbury, Ruskin, Tennyson and H. M. Stanley; and Sir John Millais flattered her by discussing the finer points of that art of portraiture which had produced such masterpieces as "Bubbles" and "Cherry Ripe". Mary interested herself in all the main religious and political movements of the day. Her contacts with the under-privileged of the Thames Valley in the wake of Mary Adelaide stimulated her thoughts in the direction of London's East End, that abyss of poverty, where an official inquiry in 1888 unearthed the squalors of labour 'sweating'. Mary read the published accounts of the Royal Commission with mounting concern and indignation. All this reading, all the social studies, proved that she had "a soul above buttons", in her mother's quaint phrase; and Mary Adelaide now applied her considerable talent to the question of providing her 'Mayflower' with a bridegroom. None of the

German princilians could be expected to marry her because of the lack of the requisite number of blue corpuscles and, a greater disadvantage, could not count upon any substantial dowry. That Mary had made up her mind not to marry a German was beside the point. Germans were sounded out, all in vain. The Queen applied the usual empirical tests. May and Dolly were summoned to Balmoral and subjected to first-hand scrutiny. After raising her eyes much to the heavens the Queen secured the approval of The Beloved One for Mary's union with the Heir Apparent, the Duke of Clarence. There was much to be said for allying her weak and effeminate grandson Eddy with a young princess whom she found to be not only "very pretty" but also a superior kind of girl considering her ancestry.

In fairness to the Queen it must be noted that in her later years she dismissed the 'tainted blood' theory, especially when it had become obvious that the tragic haemophilia was the unpalatable result in her own family of the royal inbreeding imposed by Hanoverian exclusivity. Eddy was weedy and sallow, fickle in matters of the heart, and something of a coxcomb with his waxed moustache and middle parting and quiff. His whole appearance was lethargic and willowy, and his father, from whose rough badinage no member of the family ever felt secure, called him 'Collars and Cuffs', a description which a thin neck and skinny wrists did little to challenge. A few weeks after the Balmoral visit Mary travelled to Malvern with her family and inspected Worcester Cathedral. There she saw the tomb of Arthur, the elder brother of Henry VIII. It proved to be an omen.

At the end of 1891 Eddy proposed to May in Madame de Falbe's boudoir at Luton Hoo, the home of the Danish Minister, and the nuptials were arranged for 27th February 1892. But in January the fatal influenza virus struck at Sandringham, where a grand house party had been planned to celebrate the Heir Apparent's twenty-eighth birthday. The Duke of Teck unavailingly proposed his health. Eddy was stricken. He fell into a delirium, shouting hoarsely of Lord Salisbury and Lord Randolph Churchill; but the name which burst most often from his parched lips was Hélène, from which it appeared that his true love was still the exiled Roman Catholic Princess of Orleans, whom he had been forced to reject after a Papal intervention. On his death Mary grieved more for the Queen and Princess Alexandra than for herself, for there is little doubt that she was not really in love with her fiancé. At this distance of time she emerges as the reluctant party to an arranged marriage. The Queen, although she had been a moving spirit in the romance, afterwards told George Cambridge that Mary really loved George all the time, but there is no evidence that George reciprocated her affection then. When Eddy was buried at St. George's Chapel his fiancé ordered that a bead wreath inscribed with the one word 'Hélène' should rest on his tomb, where his effigy resembled "a noble young knight at rest after the cruel battle with death", so Mary Adelaide thought.

"The nation's grief resembles that on the death of the Princess Charlotte," wrote Mr. Gladstone, who would have been about 8 years old at that unhappy time. Even as Victoria mourned—'a wedding with bright hopes turned into a funeral'—the hopes of the nation rested upon George, now a figure of high constitutional importance as the only surviving son of the Wales family. Should anything happen to him, and he had almost succumbed to that bout of typhoid, a situation fraught with unthinkable possibilities would face the Crown. Next in the succession stood George's eldest sister, the Princess Royal; but Louise had married a commoner, and if she could inherit the throne so, too, could the morganatic son of George Cambridge at some distant date. It was a prospect too harrowing, for failing Princess Louise it would have to be Princess Victoria, a spinster. Commonsense and prudence dictated that George should settle down speedily and stabilize the succession. With whom?

Mary was expected to disappear into retirement, even to some Protestant convent, and spend the rest of her natural life brooding upon her lost love. The Princess of Wales and her daughters buttered her with affection and, when the date of her cancelled wedding arrived, they carried her off to the Duke of Devonshire's place near Eastbourne. It seemed useless for the distrait Duke of Teck to cry, "There must be a Czarevitch!" every time he drew attention to the marriage of Alexandra's sister Dagmar to the future Alexander III when death removed her original fiancé, his elder brother Nicholas; but the women members of the Royal Family came slowly to realize that there could indeed be "a Czarevitch". The Tecks shepherded their daughter to the Riviera, where George was staying with his family. But the death of Eddy

In this charming study, when she was 6 years old, the future Queen Mary looked much like Little Miss Muffet

Princess Mary Adelaide, Duchess of Teck, with her family: the future Queen Mary, Adolphus ('Dolly'), Francis (Frank) and, in sailor suit, Alexander George ('Alge')

(*Left*) As Duke and Duchess of York with Queen Victoria at Osborne in 1893 on their honeymoon. (*Below*) Queen Mary as Princess of Wales at Abergeldie in 1906 with her family. In the perambulator (right) is her youngest son, Prince John. This is one of the rare photographs in which he appeared. He died at the age of 13.

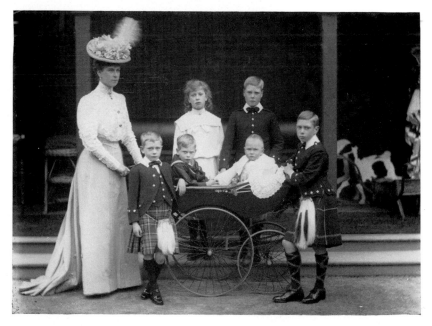

had recharged Alexandra's possessiveness. No woman should part her from her surviving son.

"*Nothing and nobody* can or shall ever come between me and my darling Georgie boy."

If George were to marry the Queen's choice must be respected, and the Queen's choice had fallen upon Marie, the eldest daughter of Victoria's second son Alfred of Edinburgh and his Romanov wife, the Grand Duchess Marie. The Prince himself responded to the stimuli of Marie's brains and beauty. Unhappily she did not respond to the bearded young man with the rather loud voice and the 'pretty' lips. Eventually she married the King of Rumania, made her niche in history as 'Missy', and in view of what happened in the Balkans probably regretted her dismissal of George.

It was 'rot', the Prince told himself, to fancy that he was in love with Marie, especially as the Prince of Wales was bantering him about the admirable qualities of Princess May. Three weeks passed before he called on the Tecks at their Cannes villa. Daily visits to 'dear Miss May' followed. Their mutual loss bound them more closely; Mary quite understood when George tearfully recalled Eddy—"my darling boy". Reports of an attachment between them reached England, by which time the Tecks had removed May to Germany. One night in Stuttgart, at the Würrtemberg *schloss*, the curtains above a window desk where Mary Adelaide was writing letters caught fire from an oil lamp. Mary kept the flames at bay with water from a ewer until the fire brigade arrived and created an assessor's fantasy by dowsing everything. "I hear you nearly burned the house down," wrote George. His sense of humour appealed to her. He could be very droll.

The Queen created him Duke of York. She disliked the title because of the reprehensible example of James II; but it was perhaps better than her first fancy, Duke of London, so very unroyal: traditionary influences must be upheld. One other problem required immediate attention. With Marie's rejection of George the only reasonable alternative was May, but the Queen's grandson could scarcely marry into a family whose insolvency was proverbial, even inscrutable. Victoria appointed an accountant to manage the Teck finances. Having gone so far the Queen paused. Alexandra's feelings should not be overridden. After his brother's death George had left the Navy to be prepared for his new responsibilities as Heir Apparent. The quarter deck was

11

exchanged for the lecture room at Heidelberg University; but his German had not significantly improved, and he learned little that he did not know already, when his mother beckoned him to Greece, where she could monopolize his filial devotion. In the Aegean spring of 1893 he could relax and reflect . . . and possibly forget May. Did he love her? Alexandra thought not. Yet he could not exclude her from his mind. Memories lingered on of their joint visit to Eddy's tomb on the anniversary of his death the previous January. He irresolutely fingered the tiepin she had given him for Christmas and wrote her a letter. Then another, followed by others. In April he returned home. All he needed was a sign.

This came from his sister Louise. The Duke of York was lured to tea at the Fifes' house near Richmond on 2nd May. By pre-arrangement Mary simultaneously arrived to "see the baby", the infant Princess Maud named for her aunt. Gently encouraged by his sister to show May the frogs in the garden pond, George decided that May was far more attractive and he proposed on the spot. The Crown Princess of Prussia was much depressed by the betrothal, for she had earmarked her nephew for one of the German princesses. It was all very melancholy, especially as she had detected in May some want of 'heart' in her dealings with small children. The Princess of Wales ominously delayed her return from Athens until after the engagement was announced on 3rd May.

"Not only by birth, but by education and by domicile, she belongs to England," rejoiced the *Morning Post*. "She possesses every qualification for the high place that awaits her." Praise indeed from the organ of the butler's pantry. But high place it was. With little effort on her part, although through the unsleeping exertions of the Cambridges, Mary became the third lady in the land after the Queen and the Princess of Wales. *The Times* viewed the engagement as a "most appropriate and delicate medicament for a wound in its nature never wholly effaceable", and the leader writer was not far short of the mark when he suggested that a "union rooted in painful memories might prove happy beyond the common lot".

In the mellow permissiveness of advancing age, the Queen withdrew the veto she had imposed upon Edward and Alexandra, and George and Mary were married in the Chapel Royal of sacred

memory on 6th July 1893 in "perfectly awful" heat. The Queen
was in a state of rare euphoria and, more by design than accident,
arrived at the chapel first instead of last, and insisted on taking her
seat immediately, to the consternation of the ushers, so that she
could measure the effect of her presence on the arriving guests.
Geraldine Somerset sourly criticized the bride's gown. Mary had
discarded the orange blossoms she was to have worn for her
wedding to Eddy, and her train was of silver and white brocade
quietly embroidered with rose, shamrock and thistle. The veil in
which Mary Adelaide had been married was far too short for
Geraldine's taste; she also belittled the bride's mother, whose
triumph was the greatest since she had 'dragged' Franz to the
altar. And what were the emotions of the Princess of Wales to
hear the responses uttered not by her darling Eddy but by his
younger brother! Too horrible!!! Otherwise the arrangements
were perfection, and Geraldine thought the police were wonderful
in their control of a crowd even larger, it was estimated, than the
great Jubilee assemblies.

The choice of York Cottage, with its cramped but cosy quarters,
was a quirk of the bridegroom. The small rooms reminded him
of his cabin aboard ship. The cottage, formerly used by bachelor
guests at Sandringham, was a wedding gift from the Prince of
Wales. Peace and quiet seemed assured; a short-lived illusion.
With the regularity of a solstice Alexandra and the 'whispering
sisters' descended upon the honeymooners. The Princess of Wales
re-arranged the furnishings, skilfully assisted by the princesses,
who sibilantly simpered behind the bride's back. Even Louise,
despite the decisive part she had played in the romance, found
time to criticize May's "poor Würrtemberg hands". Alexandra
never wholly relaxed her grip on George. Even when he commanded rough sailors aboard Her Majesty's ships she had sent
him "a great big kiss for your lovely little face", although like
Shakespeare's soldier he was still "full of strange oaths, and
bearded like the pard". Only gradually did the Princess of Wales
resign herself to the fact that her 'Georgie boy' belonged to
another woman, but it was clear to Mary from the start, in
the words of a biographer, Mr. Gore, that she had married into a
mutual admiration society. Her mother's slapdash habits, her
mother-in-law's vagueness, spurred her to practise thrift where
Mary Adelaide was prodigal and to establish order where

Alexandra, to say the least, had been imprecise. She also differed from her mother-in-law in that she harboured no personal prejudice against Wilhelm II; rather she felt that the Imperial *folie de grandeur* exposed monarchy to the ribaldry of anti-royalists.

The Yorks occupied the 'glum' York Cottage for the first eight years of their married life, and five of their six children were born there. The renamed York House at St. James's Palace became their town residence, but they felt uneasy in its gloomy and airless spaces. Buckingham Palace was prepared for the arrival of Mary's first baby, but the torrid summer of 1894 dictated a prudent escape to White Lodge, much to the gratification of Mary Adelaide, who had resolved to keep her 'precious chick' under her own wing. George found it all too trying. The fidgety ways of Maria, as he called his mother-in-law, rasped his not always urbane temper. The Home Secretary, Mr. Asquith, called to see the child when he was born on 23rd June. Three days later the Queen and members of the Royal Family with their suites arrived in a special train from Windsor. 'Aunt Queen', with three heirs living, was again in an unaccustomed state of geniality. How safe this continuity made the monarchy, so different from the lot of poor President Carnot of France, who had just been struck down by an assassin.

The Queen was delighted to find Mary nursing "a very fine strong Boy, a pretty Child". Devoutly she wished him to be called Albert, but the parents were stubborn for Edward in commemoration of the Duke of Clarence. Finally he was provided with twelve godparents and seven names—Edward Albert Christian George Andrew Patrick David. As a potential Prince of Wales he was to answer to the last name, David. At the age of two months he was left in the charge of nurses and the faithful Bricka, and Mary travelled as 'Lady Killarney' to St. Moritz with her family—they met Robert Browning there—while the Duke of York savoured the nautical delights of Cowes. Possibly the Empress Frederick was right when she divined that Mary, outwardly at any rate, nurtured no great passion for little ones, for how could she leave a baby so young?

All had been restored to normal, the travellers home and "tutsome baby"—Alexandra's endearment—gaining weight, when in October the Czar Alexander III died and George sailed to Russia for the funeral of his uncle and the marriage of 'Nicky' and 'Alicky' in the Winter Palace. He felt the separation keenly;

it made him quite ill. He could not wait to get back to Sandringham, to resume the country life, the domestic round. The Yorks drifted quietly upon the stream of life, they did not mingle with the racegoing 'Marlbocracy', the Princess of Wales regarded Sandringham as her inviolable domain, resenting any trespass by her daughter-in-law on her preserves, and the Queen herself was now appearing more in public. The future George VI was born on 20th December 1895 and Mary Adelaide rhymed rapturously: *"A Boy!!! What joy!!!"* He entered the world on the 'day of all days', the thirty-fourth anniversary of his great-grandfather's death, a day sacred to the Queen, when she and the Royal Family stood reverently before the tomb of The Beloved One at Frogmore. Little Bertie's unwelcome intrusion upon 'Mausoleum Day' was forgiven, for the child was named after the Prince Consort.

Tragedy now cast a long, low shadow over the Tecks. Shortly before Bertie's birth the Duke had lost his surviving sister Claudine, who grieved herself into the grave after the death of her inseparable sister Amélie the previous year. Happiness was briefly restored when his eldest son, Mary's favourite brother Dolly, an Army officer, married the daughter of the multi-millionaire Duke of Westminster. The second son, Frank, was less fortunate; he was shipped to India. Possibly the Tecks pushed their luck too hard, for, having seen two of their children rise to the highest positions of rank and favour, they aspired to marry Frank to George's youngest sister, Maud, who was certainly not ill-disposed towards him. Unfortunately, he had inherited not only the good nature of his mother but also her defects as an investor. As he added gambling debts to other extravagances—he was an inveterate *boulevardier* and 'lady killer', in the current phrase—he soon gathered more creditors than friends. His sister came to the rescue when he incontinently wagered £10,000 on a ridiculous bet when he probably could not have raised 10,000 pence. His debts were settled, at the price of exile to India. There he suffered acutely, for India never impressed him as it was to impress his sister. Dante's Inferno in Frank's estimation had much to commend it compared with the sub-continent, and he was glad when, having purged his offence, he was permitted to return to London. He was unchanged. 'Uncle Frank' ran up bills on his parents' charge accounts at the London stores, largely to provide numerous and costly presents for his young relations, who adored him. An estrangement grew between him and his sister. These trials were of short duration. His health deteriorated. During his last years he placated the family by undertaking works of charity. He was reconciled with Mary, but did not live to see her crowned queen. In 1910 he died at the age of 39 after an operation.

The waywardness of Frank added to the Duchess of York's burdens in the closing years of the old century. By 1896 the decline in Mary Adelaide's constitution, and her husband's increasing debility, aroused alarm. The Duchess was now expecting her third child. London bustled with preparations for the Diamond Jubilee, but White Lodge was overcast with anxiety about Mary Adelaide and Teck's mental collapse: he laughed about nothing and could not find his words. Mary gave birth to Princess Mary on 25th April. Meanwhile the surgeons decided to operate on Mary Adelaide. When Mary celebrated her thirtieth birthday her mother seemed to have recovered and was eagerly anticipating the Jubilee. Again, as on so many other ceremonial occasions, she nearly 'stole the show' from the Queen. Her progress to St. Paul's was another superb triumph. The cheers of the great crowd, mingled with genuine relief and joy at her recovery, were music in her ears. But she was in pain, and the spectacle of her poor husband wandering around the rooms at White Lodge chuckling to himself eroded her spirits.

"Oh, I don't want to die," she wept. "My children, my husband, need me."

It did not help that at this time a charity bazaar in Paris went up in flames, burning to death a German princess and other friends of the Royal Family. With dark forebodings the Yorks left for Ireland after the Jubilee, and there was talk about their acquiring a permanent home there; but such proposals, as has been seen, were anathema to the Queen and she promptly quashed this one. Mary Adelaide lingered on for another two months before her death, in October, after a second operation. The Duke of Teck pottered out the rest of his life under male nurses. When he died in the first month of the new century his three sons were serving in South Africa. He was buried beside Mary Adelaide at Windsor, and as the coffin slid into the royal vault the aged George Cambridge bent over his walking-stick and wept.

Family affairs devolved upon Mary, with much useful advice

from Aunt Augusta and with the compassion and sympathy of her husband and the Queen. At 80 Victoria was almost blind, but she insisted on attending to state business through a surprising intermediary, her youngest daughter Beatrice. 'Little Bee' read out all the important Foreign Office and other Government telegrams and documents to her mother, and with more perseverance than knowledge interpreted such intricacies of public policy as the Eastern Question and the Irish Problem. Lamentable misunderstandings sometimes resulted, but the Queen pursued her indomitable way, the Government survived, and the British Empire, a little tarnished, rode out the storm of the Boer War, in the middle of which the future Duke of Gloucester was born. Willy was enchanted to sponsor Henry, Mary's third son; another godparent was Lord Roberts, the hero of the hour. A future queen was also born in the same year, 1900—that Elizabeth of Glamis whose life story is traced in *Thirty Years a Queen*.

The Queen, with her unabated suspicions of the 'smart set', discovered in Mary those qualities lacking in others closer to her in blood and age. Some members of the Royal Family criticized the Duke of York's wife as a fuddy-duddy who disapproved of fashionable society and seemed more interested in the seamy side of life, but Victoria saw in the future Queen Consort a reflection of her own image.

"Only give me the chance," Mary told Bricka, "& I will do things as well as anybody—after all, why shouldn't I?"

The Queen agreed. Mary had relied upon her more heavily than she was aware until the blinds were drawn for the last time at Osborne. God help us all, she prayed, as Victoria slipped away to join The Beloved One forty years after the heart-rending farewell at Windsor. "The thought of England without the Queen is dreadful even to think of." George automatically became Heir Apparent and Duke of Cornwall (as well as of York), but his father's delay in creating him Prince of Wales ruffled his *amour propre*. The King had a good point; he had been Prince of Wales so long that the sudden appearance of his son bearing the same title would have caused public confusion. Already letters intended for Mary were misdirected to Alexandra. The title was not conferred until the King's birthday on 9th November 1901 after the Duke and Duchess of Cornwall and York had completed a brilliant visit to the new Dominion of Australia, with side visits to New Zealand, Canada and Cape Colony. Travel on that scale, Mary thought, was "too wonderful", but the long separation from the children nearly "killed" her.

The tour proved less arduous than the 'musical chairs' of the King and Queen at Buckingham Palace and Windsor and of the new Prince and Princess of Wales at Marlborough House. The King unreasonably objected when Mary ordered a substantial redecoration of Marlborough House designed to obliterate the last traces of the 'Marlbocracy'; she refused the King's offer of Osborne. The King grumbled but finally deferred to his daughter-in-law's judgement. She still stood in awe of him, but in matters of home-making hers was the superior intellect. The ways of the new incumbents of the throne were not hers and, although grandparental interference was endured, she and George and *her* 'chicks' kept much to themselves.

12

'Darby and Joan'

MODERN psychologists believe that George and Mary took too little trouble to understand their children. Whereas Edward and Alexandra spoiled the grandchildren, their son and his wife wished to see a return to sound Victorian educational standards and moral behaviour. Implicit obedience was exacted from the sons. Disobedience brought instant retribution. It seemed as though in rooting out the bad they sometimes overlooked the good in their offspring. The truth was, as Mary said, that she and her husband were 'wonderfully suited to each other', as had been proved during the seven and a half months of their colonial tour. Her uxorious husband "thanked God every day" for such a wife. There were times when the children seemed to interpose a barrier between them and their 'Darby and Joan' attitude to marriage. Consequently they committed blunders over their sons' training which, except in degree, differed little from the academic extremism which made George III's sons what they became and was incredibly repeated by Victoria and the Prince Consort in the case of Edward. Royal history might have followed a smoother course in the 1930s had Mary shown more insight into the child mind and had George occasionally descended from the quarter-deck and applied the large rather than the small lens of the paternal telescope to his sons. No doubt his bark was worse than his bite, but it scared the young. Constant carping bred furtive defiance. Possibly the Prince of Wales loved his family too anxiously, but the academic straitjacket prescribed by his advisers could not have been less suitable, certainly for a personality as headstrong as David.

Bitter was the reckoning, but it would be unfair to blame the shortcomings of education alone for the Abdication, for the family absorbed culture from their 'bookish' mother. There were other contributory factors, not least the father's refusal to appreciate how rapidly the world was changing. As he could not put back the clock he expected things to remain as they were, at least; and his loud eruptions of irritation did little to reconcile any of his sons to the 'old ways'. Perhaps the greatest mistake was to deprive them of boyhood contact with other young people of their age. Only the younger sons were sent to public schools, and then under duress.

The 'stinking age' of the motor-car, the increasing roar of metropolitan traffic, revolted the Heir Apparent and his wife, but Mary created a quiet haven at Marlborough House. The family moved there in the spring of 1903. Sheltered behind a stout brick wall from the stares of the throng in The Mall, the Wales family enjoyed sunny summer days in the garden, where the children were enjoined to play their ball games 'quietly', while George read and Mary wrote. It was hard to be torn out of this "truly domestic scene" to entertain Ascot guests or to support the Head of State at the glittering Court ceremonials which had too swiftly succeeded the discreet solemnities of Victoria's régime. They escaped to their new Scottish home at Abergeldie Castle near Balmoral after the coronation, and May gave birth to her fifth child, the future Duke of Kent, at Sandringham at the end of Coronation Year. Sometimes she and George slipped away from their young 'regiment' of children to Switzerland—anywhere to be alone together.

"How we do travel about to be sure!" remarked Mary after a series of official and private peregrinations during the next few years, including another visit to the Court of Vienna, which made even the Victorian way of life look hedonistic. The ageing Franz Josef had become an austere host. He dined at five in the evening, retired at eight and, rising at four o'clock in the morning, had completed a day's work before breakfast. Further overseas visits were suspended until after the birth of Prince John in the summer of 1905. He was the last of the 'regiment' and an epileptic, destined to spend a brief tormented life under the care of nurses on a Sandringham farm. He died in 1919 at the age of 13.

In the autumn after John's birth came the memorable adventure of India, parting them from the family for nearly six months. India made an unforgettable impression on the Princess of Wales —"when I die India will be written on my heart". Her second son was to be the last Emperor of India; she would have found that unbelievable then. Cairo offered hospitality on the way home, but the visit lacked the splendour of Alexandra's famous encounter with the pashas. They were joined in Greece by the King and Queen and Princess Victoria. In Athens, as in other historic cities on this and later tours, Mary invariably stole away to inspect art treasures and ancient remains, a taste so sophisticated that George usually begged to be excused from accompanying her.

Victoria Eugenie, the daughter of 'Little Bee', now flashed upon the scene with a brilliant but trouble-scarred marriage to Alfonso XIII, the last King of Spain before the revolution of 1931. If there was one thing more calculated to provoke royal discord than a morganatic union it was a match between a Roman Catholic and a Protestant. 'Ena' had taken instruction in the Roman faith. The very idea panicked Aunt Augusta, who was also mortified beyond expression when the Spanish king and his fiancée frivolously endangered themselves by driving in a motor-car at Biarritz. But Mary had been devoted to Ena from childhood and, all objections having been overruled, she and the Prince of Wales attended the wedding in Madrid. An uninvited guest was the anarchist Morales, who tossed a bomb at the bridal procession on its return journey from the cathedral. The explosion killed many spectators, and Ena's bridal gown was splashed with their blood. The King, apart from losing his orders, smitten from his breast by a bomb splinter, escaped unhurt. "A most unpleasant experience," wrote Mary. Otherwise she enjoyed her introduction to the Spanish Court, which was even more feudal than the Viennese, although she could never forget poor Ena, trembling in trauma, constantly repeating, "I saw a man without any legs!"

Next came a yachting trip to Norway with Princess Mary for the coronation of King Haakon and Queen Maud. There followed the last of their series of Continental roamings, to Berlin and Paris; for soon Mary was writing: "God help us!" The brief reign of Edward VII had ended and George had lost his "best friend & the best of fathers". As King he would now look to "darling May" as his never failing help and comfort.

Public opinion and the older aristocracy welcomed the new reign as a return, in the words of Sir Harold Nicolson, to "the more sober English standards of felicity". The marriage of the new monarchs was founded upon rock. But between the accession and the King's 'new position' in May 1910 and the coronation thirteen months later they were exposed to the sudden sharp pinch of scandal. Few people, appreciating the solid middle-class qualities of the new incumbent to the throne, took seriously a libellous fiction that he had contracted a bigamous marriage; but the King felt obliged at once to confute the charge and confound its perpetrator.

In 1893 the *Star* newspaper had alleged that in 1890, before his marriage, he had wed the daughter of an English admiral in Malta. It might have been as well to have slain this canard then, but the country was still agog over the Tranby Croft affair and nothing was done. As the story had never been denied a journalist, Edward Mylius, rehashed the 'facts' for the delectation of the readers of a subversive Paris tract, *The Liberator*. Normally scant attention was paid to anti-monarchist effusions in the foreign Press, but George determined to destroy the "abominable lie" in the full light of day. Mylius was prosecuted for criminal libel before Lord Chief Justice Alverstone, and the King was ready to stand in the witness-box and state the true position: that at the time of the alleged marriage he had not been in Malta. The lady he was supposed to have married had been presented to him only twice—once when she was a girl of 8 and again after she had happily married somebody else. But, unlike any other member of the Royal Family, the Sovereign cannot testify in the Sovereign's court of law. As long ago as the Wars of the Roses a man convicted of treason was released because the only testimony against him was that of the King himself. Advice on those lines was given by the jurist who became Viscount Simon and Lord Chancellor, and Rufus Isaacs instead read a statement signed by the King in which he denied the whole fabrication. The "scoundrel Mylius", as Mary branded him, was sentenced to a year's imprisonment.

This "unpleasant occurrence" was soon forgotten, but the early months of the reign brought the Queen other problems. It was said that she tried to 'boss' the King; conversely, that he intimidated her. Truth lay somewhere between. Her attitude was that the King must reign, and in order to reign he must be sheltered from the importunities of daily life, certainly from favour-seekers and even from the children. She was always to draw a firm line between the King's duties as Head of State and as *paterfamilias*. Heavy responsibilities burdened her shoulders, including the transfer of the *ménage* from Marlborough House to Buckingham Palace, which she energetically transformed. Not her least worry was the interference of Queen Alexandra, who not only proved troublesome about matters of Court precedence but also was an unconscionable time moving her 'things' back into Marlborough House.

In almost every respect the Queen was the antithesis of her mother-in-law, not least in fashion. Her flair for colour came from her Hungarian grandmother. Where Alexandra appeared in brilliant raiment her daughter-in-law presented a stylish figure in delicate pastel shades; conspicuous rather than sparkling where 'Darling Motherdear' was all bird of paradise. Matrons copied Mary's toques: they were dictated by her husband's conservatism. Wide-brimmed hats were not to his taste. Indeed, her choice of apparel reflected his rather than her preference. Almost violently opposed to change, he resented more than anything constant fluctuations of fashion. With minor modifications the Queen dressed in much the same way as she had done when they were engaged.

Official biographies of George V and Queen Mary maintain a cryptic silence about Mary's attitude to the parliamentary crisis of 1911, the first great challenge to the monarchy since the Reform agitation eighty years before. The Queen, the most politically acute of the three consorts recalled in this volume, was certainly not impervious to the threat. On the whole she favoured a more democratic approach to the realities. Industrial unrest was the child, not of extreme welfarism as it became at the other extreme fifty years later, but of abysmal poverty and unemployment; not of a system which permitted teenagers to earn more than their parents, sometimes for 'dead-end' work, and labouring wives to demand professional equality with their husbands and sons, but of male breadwinners who knew that if they fell sick 1,000 workless would step into their jobs. That was the root cause of the cry "Peers *versus* People", and Mary, with her growing interest in social problems, had plenty to say about it privately. She never obtruded her views upon the King, who had inherited the reform controversy from his father. "How I hate politics!" Alexandra had declared, overlooking how forcibly she had expressed herself about Schleswig-Holstein. The difference between Mary and her predecessors, especially Adelaide, is that she carefully avoided involvement in the crisis—that is, through the unrestrained gossip of courtiers and the writers of pasquinades. What she did not say the 'little ears' of the Court could not repeat.

Industrial strikes followed the parliamentary wrangle—"one tiresome thing after another". For suffragettes Mary had no sympathy, as has been noted; she had probably never heard of Mr. Mill's oration. Her robust femininity maintained that while Woman might reign over her own domestic province, the last word remained with Man. The King was the King. "Idiotic short-sighted women" such as Mrs. Emmeline Pankhurst exasperated her, as did all those other well-bred women trying to starve themselves to death in jail. But during the next three years the suffragettes carried their standard to the very gates of Buckingham Palace. Mr. Bloomfield, an architect, was horrified when his daughter Mary at an investiture knelt before the King shrieking, "Your Majesty, won't you stop torturing women?" It was a novel thought for the King, a kindly man beneath the crust of regal formality. The Queen seemed carved out of ice while the offender was removed. "Very unpleasant," she noted later. How very 'tiresome' was this question of votes for women.

She was as much on her guard against suffragettes as she had been against tigers in India during her second visit to the subcontinent with the King in the winter of 1911 for the most magnificent and the last of the three Durbars, the first two having been carried out by Edward VII as Prince of Wales and later as Emperor. George V and Queen Mary were the first reigning monarchs jointly to receive the direct personal homage of the Indian princes and peoples. Mary was as much Empress of India as Alexandra and Victoria had been, but the constitutional point was helpfully raised by the manufacturers of a popular brand of soap for advertising purposes and satisfactorily confirmed; indeed, Mary became and remained Dowager Empress of India until the *Raj* dissolved in 1947. The decision of the British government to create a new administrative capital in Delhi inspired Hindu soothsayers to prophesy that such pride would bring about a great fall; thirty-six years later they were proved correct. Tiger hunting had more appeal for the King than visits to places of historical interest, and, after renewing the romance of her 1905 tour with an inspection of the Taj Mahal and other temples, the Queen followed the guns into the jungle, where she perched in a tree and started to knit. One tiger made straight for the tree and gazed up at her with predacious yearning.

"Look, Lord Shaftesbury—a tiger!"

But Shaftesbury was too late, and the beast, outstared by the Queen-Empress, padded out of sight and range. During their earlier tour the royal visitors had had to change into mourning for King Christian. Now their homecoming was dampened by mourning for the Duke of Fife. "A fresh trial for Motherdear", sighed the Queen; and after the memorial service for "poor dear Macduff" at St. Paul's she pondered: "Such is life & one must make the best of it."

Class war at home had meanwhile entered a sharp and sinister phase. Trade unionism grappled militantly with the forces of capital. Strikes in the coalfields threatened the nation's life's blood. The Queen thought the discontent sprang from the Liberal government's kid-gloved handling of the rising Labour movement. She and the King resolved to see things for themselves. The decision set a useful precedent for their successors. The spectacle of the monarch condescending to exchange pleasantries with coal-grimed pit lads, and the Queen poking about inside the tied cottages of the industrial poor in areas where royalty had never been seen before, acted as a deterrent to civil strife on a larger scale, although the discontent rumbled on. The baton charges of the mounted constabulary against stone-throwing miners, and too frequent appeals to the military in the colliery districts, reflected the intellectual bankruptcy of the elected representatives of the people, who seemed to be doing little to justify their £400 per Member per year, a munificent sum to most of their constituents.

If the scene at home was disquieting, abroad the outlook was positively alarming. An attempt was made on the Kaiser's life at Karlsruhe in 1913. Distrust of the rising War Lord's intentions was no excuse for the King to refuse an invitation to Berlin soon afterwards for the wedding of Wilhelm's only daughter, Victoria Louise, to a nephew of Queen Alexandra. The marriage ended the feud between the Hohenzollerns and the Brunswicks which had darkened relations since Prussia's seizure of Hanover in 1866, but it did nothing to halt the headlong rush towards Armageddon. This was the last gathering of the 'royal mob'. Most of its members were destined either for the assassin's bullet or for exile. War still seemed improbable as 1914 dawned, and the Queen prayed that "the clouds over these dear Islands may disperse". In April came her first state visit as Queen to a foreign republic. Paris was perfect, the chestnuts in flower, the crowds friendly; she disagreed with Aunt Augusta's stricture that the French were a nation of regicides, although she missed the familiar pleasure of being able to relax among royal relations. She was depressed by the apparent slump in British prestige abroad, but had recovered her spirits when the French President returned the visit.

The significance of the assassination of Archduke Franz Ferdinand and his morganatic wife the Duchess of Hohenberg at Sarajevo in July was not immediately apparent. The King and Queen deplored the family and dynastic consequences of the tragedy—"dreadful for the poor old Emperor", noted the Queen; but as events raced out of control she fervently hoped the world would not go to war for the sake of "tiresome Servia". Hope turned to ashes. Within a few months Queen Mary was virtually commanding that "monstrous regiment of women" whose war work became an indispensable concomitant of final victory. She sounded the right note.

"I know that I am expressing what is felt by thousands of wives and mothers," she said in a message to the armed forces, "when I say that we are determined to help one another in keeping your homes ready against your glad homecoming." It was her purpose to ensure that the chaotic disorganization of the women's effort during the Boer War was not repeated.

The Queen's whole life now seemed to have been a preparation for her finest hour. Her social studies, her contacts with the 'Labour women', yielded a harvest of goodwill vital to the nation's resolve. Her official biographer neatly summed up the role of the King and Queen in the war with the comment that they felt more at their ease with British working people than they ever had with London Society or foreign royalties. The workers were still in

(*Above*) Queen Mary emerging from a Welsh coalmine in 1912 without a feather out of place, and (*below*) as regal as ever on the footplate of a Great Western Railway locomotive driven into Swindon by King George V in 1924

Pearls . . . as only Queen Mary knew how to wear them.
She was then in her sixtieth year

ferment in August 1914. Not the least disagreeable element in this situation was the extent of unemployment among women. Queen Mary conceived it her priority to engage this wasted womanpower in useful war work so as to release men for the Front, to ensure that they were fairly paid and, especially in the munitions factories, protected by maximum safeguards. In the military field she helped to break down prejudice against 'women soldiers'—the idea of women in uniform!—and supported the dignity of the Women's Legion by assuming leadership of the Women's Army Auxiliary Corps which grew out of it.

She made her greatest impact in the industrial sphere in association with the militant Mary Macarthur, who as secretary of the Women's Trade Union League had by a brilliant display of demagogic ardour and bustling reformism visibly improved the status of women. Mary was a 'Red', a kind of female counterpart of Keir Hardie, founder of the Labour movement, the Florence Nightingale of women and children in the sweated industries. For all her energy, thousands of women had no work when the war broke out and many of those in jobs toiled for a pittance. Now they had to face competition from middle-class or titled women all too eager to knit and sew for the men at the Front. The Old Contemptibles were still landing in France when the Queen, perceiving the injustice of the situation, demanded action to place the whole women's effort on a practical national footing. Through one of her household staff, Lady Bertha Dawkins, she pestered the Government, whose evasions angered her. Before the end of the first war month the Central Committee on Women's Employment had been firmly established with a 'mixed bag' of celebrities ranging from Margaret Bondfield (who became Britain's first woman Minister) and Susan Lawrence to Lady Crewe and Mrs. Austen Chamberlain.

Women were channelled through model workshops and training centres; work was shared out; and throughout the land women felt that they were at least being treated as more than cogs in a machine. When Lady Crewe brought Mary Macarthur and the Queen together the two women reached an almost immediate understanding. They shared a capacity for hard work. Mary Macarthur's knowledge of the working class derived from painful first-hand experience, the Queen's from insight supported

12

by her own penetrating analysis of industrial conditions, supplemented by catholic reading. They became close friends, surviving the suspicion of Mary Macarthur's Labour colleagues, who failed to understand that, however divided by rank and influence, the two Marys were women, and dedicated ones at that.

They learned much from each other. Miss Bondfield thought the Queen would have made an ideal factory inspector: in her simple clothes she was sometimes indistinguishable from the working women whom she visited in their homes and factories. An important by-product of their intimacy until Mary Macarthur's sudden death through overwork was that when Labour governments secured office after the war the Queen was able to put the wives of socialist Ministers at ease and to contribute as much to smooth relations as did the King in his deft handling of the Cabinet. But the Queen's influence permeated not only the Central Committee, to which the Royal Army Clothing Department yielded responsibility for the manufacture of all shirts for the Forces, but also every other wartime female activity—needlework, nursing, hospitals, munitions. Wherever women laboured in the common cause, there the Queen would be found, encouraging, suggesting, advising.

Many women in their late forties would have collapsed beneath the burdens she carried, but her stamina never failed her. Again and again she blessed her "Cambridge constitution". Someone begged her not to stand so much. "Too funny," she replied. She steeled herself against the infinite pathos of numerous visits to war wounded at Queen Mary's Hospital for the limbless at Roehampton, which dealt with the colossal figure of 20,000 amputees—and that was only half the number of men who lost limbs during the war. It almost broke her heart to see "so many men without arms, legs, eyes, etc.". As often as possible she bustled down to the East End to Queen Mary's Hospital at Stratford East. On returning from a visit to his daughter there Will Thorne, a local MP, met the Prince of Wales, who asked where he had been. "To your Ma's place, of course," he said. The institution was always known as 'Ma's place' during the Queen's lifetime.

Knitting was her refuge from the anxiety of the war reports. The Queen bottled up her emotions: she could never summon up one of Alexandra's great rages, or find release in tears as she grew older. In her conservatism Queen Mary was more English than the English. Mrs. John Clynes, the wife of a future Labour Minister, noted at Windsor how when the Queen spoke of a poison-gas victim whom she had visited her needles clicked faster and faster as she bit back her emotions. Two of her sons were serving officers, and she feared for their safety, especially as the Prince of Wales was in the habit of riding up to the front line on his bicycle, while Bertie survived the Battle of Jutland in a gun turret, by a margin which can be guessed from the fate of ships less fortunate than HMS *Collingwood*. The King's tours of the Front filled her with dread; she never felt easy when he was away. Her forebodings were not without substance, for on his second visit in the autumn of 1915 his horse reared up and rolled over on him at Hesdigneul. "Too unlucky" was all she said before she realized the extent of his injuries—a fractured pelvis. According to his official biographer the King was never quite the same again; concern for his health added to the Queen's cares. By Christmas he was making progress, and the family gathering at Sandringham was enlivened by the Queen's rendering of several popular comic songs. Her lighter moods were best described, improbably, by Keir Hardie. "When that woman laughs," he said, "she does laugh, and not make a contortion like so many royalties." A housemaid at Buckingham Palace was "taken all aback" to hear the Queen whistling ditties from musical comedy in the corridor.

Repeatedly the Queen urged the King for permission to visit France, but the opportunity did not arise until the summer of 1917. The Channel was swarming with U-boats and the King accompanied her to Calais: like William IV he would be at hand in the event of sea-sickness (the Queen did not love the sea) or worse. From a château at Montreuil she proceeded to every hospital within reach, talked to every patient, inspected the battlefields as far as Amiens, her path strewn with the pathetic discards of refugees. With the Prince of Wales she motored to Crécy, where she observed that it was probably the first time a Prince of Wales had visited the battlefield since the Black Prince fought there.

Only when victory seemed assured did the Queen relax. The Sovereign and his Consort celebrated their silver wedding in July 1918 with thanksgiving at St. Paul's and a Guildhall presentation, amid much popular rejoicing. On Armistice Day—"dull first, rain in the afternoon"—she could not but recall the stupendous sacrifice of "this ghastly war" and, thankful to see the end of it, she described it as "the greatest day in the world's history".

13

The Abdication

EUROPE of the kings lay in ruins. It did not surprise Queen Mary that the ancient thrones of the Romanovs and the Hapsburgs had been destroyed, or that Wilhelm's downfall and exile at Doorn were the price to be paid by the man who had started "this awful war". The British monarchy had survived the wreck battered but, if not stronger, certainly strong enough to withstand the magnetic attraction of President Wilson's starry-eyed republicanism. The King and Queen gratefully settled into a domestic routine which their sons, welcoming the comparative permissiveness of the 'twirling twenties', found irksome if not ridiculous. They were stay-at-home Sovereigns: in the last sixteen years of the reign they were out of the country for a total of seven weeks. Public engagements took them all over the kingdom, yet they enjoyed more leisure together than any of their married successors.

The King toiled at his 'boxes' early and late. With a glance at the clock at half-past ten at night he would indicate that it was bedtime, not only for him but for his family. He had never seen the inside of a West End night club in his life and could not comprehend the allure of Mayfair after dark which David, especially, found irresistible. Somehow the King expected life to settle back into the pre-war groove; its failure to oblige him filled him with bewilderment and dismay. Tension was increased by his failure to recognize that his sons were grown men. The King and Queen were closer to their daughter Mary before her marriage to Viscount Lascelles, a wealthy man fifteen years her senior, than to any of their sons. Bertie's relationship was warm enough, but even he was glad to seek release in marriage. With

one exception all their surviving children wed commoners.
Dynastically the range of selection was restricted after the break
with the royal houses of Germany. There were other considerations. Queen Victoria in the first flush of matrimony and motherhood bridled at the very thought of morganatic marriage—"we
would *never* wish to discuss it"; but with the passage of time her
resolution weakened, for it became obvious that royal inbreeding
tended to adulterate the blood royal. When the Queen died
haemophilia had stricken four of her grandchildren and great-
grandchildren. Her son Leopold succumbed to it. The Spanish
Bourbons were almost wiped out by the scourge, passed on
through Queen Ena. From that time the Royal Family widened
the field of marriage. In the nineteen-sixties the choice was further
extended beyond the old nobility when Princess Margaret
married outside it.

The problem was the Prince of Wales. He alone of the family
remained unmarried. Queen Mary was disturbed by his refusal to
settle down. Marriage was a subject he could never raise with his
parents. The gulf became unbridgeable. He went his way, and the
King and Queen found their chief fulfilment in their labours for
the common weal. Separation for even a few days fretted them;
to be parted for only three weeks seemed an eternity. The Queen
at least tried to keep pace with the younger generation, but the
King continued to regard the post-war era with scepticism.
When he discovered the Queen practising the tango under the
graceful direction of Sir Frederick Ponsonby, a trusted courtier,
he conveyed without repeating himself that such exercises were
unsuited to his Court.

Disappointment over the Heir Apparent's failure to accept an
approved bride gave way to "relief and joy" when Princess
Elizabeth was born at Bruton Street in 1926; she became their
favourite grandchild. 'Lilibet's' enchanting ways helped the King
back to health after his almost fatal illness in 1928. The 1920s
twice nearly brought George V to the grave. In 1925, the year of
his mother's death, a severe attack of bronchitis forced him to
take a Mediterranean cruise, but it proved a minor disaster. Toria,
who had spent much of her time nursing Queen Alexandra,
joined the royal yacht at Venice. From that time the Queen found
herself isolated by the brother and sister, whose mutual attachment created a barrier which outsiders found it almost impossible

to penetrate. If she invited them ashore in Italy for sight-seeing expeditions she invariably found herself in a minority. When by chance they were persuaded to follow her to places of historical significance in Naples, Pompeii or Sicily they ruined her pleasure by trivial family jokes. "Give me England!" said the Queen.

By modern standards the King was old for his 60 years. A succession of political crises, rising unemployment, strikes, and the onset of Ramsay MacDonald's first Labour government had exposed him to gruelling tests. Through all these the Queen was his refuge and his comforter. She understood "these Labour people", or thought she did; now she blamed, not the trade unions but appalling housing conditions for social unrest. Her message to the troops at the outbreak of the war, about "keeping your homes ready against your glad homecoming", read strangely when so many families either had no homes of their own or homes which were as much a mockery of good housing norms in degree as they had been in the early years of Queen Adelaide. Queen Mary's life from then on was a mesh of cares and worries. Her favourite brother Dolly died in 1927 before he was 60, and then came the agony of the King's almost mortal illness in 1928, when from November until the following summer he hovered at death's door. It began with a week's shooting at Sandringham. When the Royal Family returned to London the King "had a chill and had to go to bed—too tiresome". Acute septicaemia developed and the King's heart began to fail. Only a miracle appears to have saved his life as the doctors probed desperately for the source of infection.

The Prince of Wales was urgently recalled from East Africa, covering the 7,000 miles home in nine days, a remarkable feat for those times. Baldwin met him at Dover. The Prince, probably surmising that his father was about to die, told the Prime Minister that he could always speak freely to him of anything. "I shall remind you of that, Sir," said Baldwin, and all at once he had a supernatural feeling that one day he would have to 'speak freely' to the Prince about a woman. Throughout this ordeal the Queen suppressed her fears. While the King was convalescing at Bognor she conducted investitures on his behalf: "business as usual". The Sovereigns celebrated the twentieth anniversary of their reign in May 1930. The nation was in the throes of the world depression and MacDonald's second Labour government tussled with unemployment as uselessly as any administration before it. In the

1931 crisis which brought the National Government to power the King's sister Louise died. The death of an old naval comrade Sir Charles Cust also grieved the King. But the worst blow was the death of the octogenarian Lord Stamfordham—'dear Bigge'— who for thirty years had been his adviser. Altogether it was "a tiresome year" for Queen Mary: 3 millions drawing the dole or 'public assistance' at home, socialist authoritarianism rampaging abroad. The early nineteen-thirties brought some recompense. The two younger sons, Kent and Gloucester, contracted happy marriages; and between their weddings came the Silver Jubilee of 1935, the first national festivity of its kind since the Victorian Jubilees. That autumn the Queen had "great fun" at the ghillies' ball at Balmoral, dancing twelve reels in succession. There was just one personal regret: David remained a bachelor and the name of Mrs. Simpson was whispered at Court.

The sun was rapidly setting on the reign. On 20th January 1936 the King died peacefully at Sandringham, seven weeks after Toria. Her death broke him up. The King had rarely opened the day's toil without exchanging a telephone confidence with his sister.

"Is that you, you damned old fool?" she said one day.

"Just a moment, Ma'am—His Majesty is just coming on the line," the palace operator replied.

The King's death "tinged the whole world's sky", in Queen Mary's words. She marked the "quite curious" coincidence that she had been at Sandringham at the death of the two brothers, Clarence and George V. Sixteen years later she was to note another 'curious' fact: she was informed of the death of her two sons, Kent in 1942 and George VI in 1952, by telephone. But now she knelt to kiss the hand of His Most Excellent Majesty Edward the Eighth by the Grace of God of Great Britain Ireland and the British Dominions beyond the Seas King Defender of the Faith Emperor of India. The new monarch was 41. Baldwin in his parliamentary tribute to George V expressed thankfulness that "even in her sorrow Queen Mary is spared to the people who love her". How close she was to their hearts, how they would treasure her not only for the King's sake but for her own! Death had sundered a "rich companionship". With grateful surprise the Queen Mother realized that people loved her for herself.

The Imperial Crown was placed on the King's coffin, but the Maltese cross above it fell into the gutter with a tinkle as the gun carriage was towed to Westminster Hall for the lying-in-state. A bad omen, the new king thought. Archbishop Cosmo Lang called on the widowed Queen and wrote presciently afterwards: "I can only be most thankful for what has been and, for what is to be, hope for the best. God guide the King!" The years had wrought great changes in Edward VIII. The Queen Mother had managed him sympathetically when he 'blew up' over the mediaeval garb which he was forced to wear at his Investiture as Prince of Wales in 1911, and after his unfruitful sojourn at Oxford University she complacently assured Aunt Augusta that he would not be bored at Neu Strelitz when perfecting his German there: he was a contented person who "never rushed about after amusement". The reverse was nearer the truth. David was restless like his grandfather. He had carried his handsome presence—"quite a pleasure to look at him", thought his mother—to the four corners of the earth; those exhausting Empire tours did much to create a sense of 'family' in the disparate dominions then so proud to call themselves British. Yet George V disparaged his son.

"People who don't know," he complained to Queen Mary, "will begin to think that he is either mad or the biggest rake in Europe, such a pity!"

This crushing judgment was provoked by the Prince's attachment to 'fads', dancing into the small hours, his appearance in original clothing which clashed with his father's ideas of modesty.

Did the eighth Edward really want to be King? The question whether he could have provided an heir to the throne is outside the scope of this volume. In the event he remained childless; the succession would have passed, sooner or later, to his brother's daughter and her heirs. A collision with the Establishment would also have created unpleasantness, even if the problem of marriage to Mrs. Simpson had not arisen. The more settled in their habits his parents had become, the more their son estranged himself from them and their Court. "Remember who you are," his father had reminded him; to which he had asked himself, "Who am I?" He developed a quality of mystical apartness, inherited ironically from the mother who so little understood him. Consequently the shock of the Abdication after his brief ten months' reign struck her with stunning force.

Since 1930 the bachelor Prince had equipped Fort Belvedere as a haven where he could be himself. If he later had any regrets about surrendering the Crown it was that he had to abandon the quaint retreat which he loved better than any of his father's mansions, and to which he was to look back in old age with nostalgia, for it was his own and perhaps only tangible creation. It is therefore surprising that Queen Mary, although the Fort was near Windsor, never visited her son until he had been settled there for nearly five years, and then only out of curiosity about Mrs. Simpson.

In the early months of the reign David treated his mother with the utmost compassion. He sensed the emptiness the King's death had left—"I miss dearest Papa quite dreadfully"—and when he was away he tried to fill the gap by corresponding regularly. He did everything to ease the pang of leaving the palace for Marlborough House, where she settled in October 1936 at the age of 68 with George V's disconsolate cairn terrier. The King returned with Mrs. Simpson from his Mediterranean cruise in the yacht *Nahlin* and, virtually shutting his brothers out of his private life, faced the future with a new Belvedere Set. Almost until the end the Queen Mother hoped this would prove but another love affair, but when she realized the depth of her son's feelings she begged him to put aside Mrs. Simpson for the sake of the country and the monarchy. How could the Sovereign take as his consort a woman who had two previous husbands living? The word 'duty' dropped like a stone on a frozen pond at a chilly interview in November. Abdication was unthinkable to a Queen with so deeply ingrained a sense of duty to the nation and Empire. Of all life's tragedies this was her most agonizing.

"A pretty kettle of fish!" she said to Baldwin. "Really—this might be Rumania!"

As the crisis gathered momentum the Queen Mother scraped up the last reserves of self-control to maintain an illusion of normality. Her toque, caressing the beautifully curled head like a diadem, bobbed in and out of Christmas stores, exhibitions, museums and art galleries and antique dealers' shops. Somebody must be seen to be at the helm. Her umbrella poked among the ruins of the Crystal Palace, lately reduced by fire to a blackened ruin—an ominous disaster in some way reflecting the peril of the monarchy, for the Prince Consort's great glass ark from Hyde

Park, reminding her of faded glories, had seemed indestructible. How had the mighty fallen!

"Rather foggy," she noted of the final day of the great ordeal. Before that day was over she had lost one king and gained another. George VI came to show her the Abdication Instrument. He burst into tears. She felt she had plumbed the very nadir of misery, and on top of everything the new queen consort Elizabeth was in bed with a cold, which turned out to be influenza, her second attack in a year. "Too unlucky." One last duty remained: to dissuade the departing king from broadcasting his farewell from the Augusta Tower at Windsor Castle. She failed. The new Duke of Windsor said his piece. Then, travelling as 'Mr. James'—a sardonic flashback to the last Stuart King—he caught a warship to France.

"Have had a good crossing," he telegraphed. "Glad to hear this morning's ceremony went off so well. Hope Elizabeth better. Best love and best of luck to you both."

Nothing could be more banal. Laurence Housman, whose *Victoria Regina* had been perennially banned by the Lord Chamberlain, had had his famous series of playlets licensed in the new reign. He summed up the situation:

"The Victorian Age is over at last. In one week the Crystal Palace has been burned down, Edward has announced that he will marry Mrs. Simpson and my plays on Queen Victoria are to be licensed."

"This morning's ceremony" was the proclamation of George VI by Garter King of Arms at St. James's Palace. The Queen Mother watched from the wardrobe room at Marlborough House beside the new king and her two granddaughters, Elizabeth and Margaret. No queen in history had seen two of her sons proclaimed King within just over 300 days or could look back over forty-five years to her own engagement to two future Sovereigns in turn, the one to die, the other now dead but whose spirit she so often invoked during "this sad year". Never would she see the Duchess of Windsor so long as she lived. Largely on her insistence the Duchess was neither welcomed to England nor permitted the style of Royal Highness. The Duke afterwards considered himself "a Southerner by marriage"; his wife hailed from Maryland. What Queen Mary would have thought one June day in 1966, when thirteen years after her death a slate plaque to her memory was unveiled at Marlborough House by her granddaughter Queen Elizabeth II, is beyond the bounds of calm conjecture; for the ceremony was carried out in the presence of the Duchess of Windsor.

From the Abdication nightmare the Queen Mother rose to the calls of public need in the new reign. Idle she could never be. The immediate business in prospect was the coronation of George VI, and she purposefully broke ancient prejudice by resolving to attend the ceremony, at which she "never looked happier or more regal". The Duke of Windsor married Mrs. Simpson in France the following month on the anniversary of George V's birthday, and the Queen Mother telegraphed her congratulations. Queen Maud's unexpected death after an operation in London eighteen months later cut the Queen Mother's last links with Queen Alexandra's family. As her surviving brother Alge, the Duke of Athlone, was soon to assume the Governor-Generalship of Canada she felt lonely and depressed.

Only three of Queen Victoria's children survived, including the old Duke of Connaught, who kept in touch with her. He had been present with Mary at the old queen's death. Very old, still very gallant, he offered his services to George VI in 1939, pointing out that field-marshals never retire. Another echo of the past travelled all the way from Holland just after the Munich crisis. The Queen Mother received a letter from ex-Kaiser Wilhelm expressing relief at the preservation of peace. He had not the slightest doubt "that Mr. N. Chamberlain was inspired by Heaven & guided by God Who took pity on His children on Earth by crowning his mission with such relieving success". More than a quarter of a century had elapsed since Queen Mary had last heard from the architect of the 'awful war', but the message touched some hidden chord. 'Poor William' must have been aghast at the thought of another war between Britain and Germany.

She preferred not to dwell on the prospect of another holocaust as, moving among her people with infinite grace and charm, she set an example of sedate calm in vivid contrast to the fervour of the times and exercised a steadying influence on a monarchy grievously undermined by the Abdication. She realized more than ever that by rejecting 'duty' her eldest son had encouraged that "hateful fiend Hitler" to believe Britain decadent and incapable of resisting his plans of European conquest and rapine For herself the Queen Mother had no fear: her physical courage complemented her mental toughness. Light was thrown on these qualities when in the summer of 1939 her limousine was struck by a heavy lorry and overturned as she was returning from Wimbledon. Bruised and shocked, the Queen Mother with her two companions, Lord Claud Hamilton and Lady Constance Milnes Gaskell, was rescued with the help of two ladders. Mr. Louis Wulff wrote: "Nothing has ever become her so well as her manner of leaving the wrecked car." An eye-witness noted that she climbed up and down the ladders as if she had been walking down steps at the Coronation, toque erect on the curled head, not one hair out of place. A flying fragment of glass missed piercing an eye. "A lucky escape," she told the King and Queen, who were visiting the United States. It was one of her masterly understatements: she was almost killed.

By the King's command, and by no desire of hers, the Queen Mother spent the war years in the Cotswolds. It was considered that an old lady of 72, however active, would be an encumbrance in London, and as Sandringham and Balmoral were in the invasion zones a retreat to the palladian mansion of the Duke of Beaufort at Badminton seemed logical and prudent. Her niece, the Duchess, was a daughter of Queen Mary's eldest brother Dolly. Leaving the Royal Family to bear the heat and burden of the war in the Metropolis was "not at all the thing", and she felt "rather useless" at first.

The five years at Badminton nevertheless proved to be among the most rewarding of her life. All varieties of war work engaged her attention, with rounds of visits to factories and evacuees, hospitals and workshops, the organization of salvage collections and relentless attacks on the all-devouring ivy which threatened Badminton's historic brickwork. She had been warned of the danger of a possible kidnapping attempt by Nazi paratroops: the exiled monarchs, Queen Wilhelmina and King Haakon had been most insistent about it. So she usually set forth on her rural expeditions with a military bodyguard, sometimes riding in a basket-chair perched on a farm cart. It looked like a tumbril.

"You never know," she told her niece. "It may come to that."

In her enthusiasm for hoarding scrap iron she sometimes picked up farm implements which had been left in the fields. They were "nice pieces of metal" which would help Lord Beaverbrook's salvage drive no end; but before they were added to her other 'loot' they were quietly returned to the owners. Collecting—of antiques—was a lifelong passion. The Queen's discriminating eye and cultivated taste evoked the admiration and even the envy of art dealers. Much of her priceless collection was removed from Marlborough House for safety to the country. Unlike Queen Alexandra, she did not collect for the sake of building up a jumble of treasures. She knew her subject and during her reign had assembled whole rooms full of matched antique furniture and *bric à brac* all in their period setting. She restored the eighteenth-century atmosphere to her London residence. Lost, missing or misplaced pieces were remorselessly tracked down. More than once she traced royal relics from having read of their existence in a book or noted their presence in a royal painting. Endless hours were spent cataloguing the matchless lumber of the centuries, and the sorting out of Mary Adelaide's and Queen Alexandra's trophies after their death taxed her expertise and challenged her ingenuity. A similar routine was observed at Badminton, where she annotated diaries and rearranged old family photographs and papers in an orderly continuity which is a tribute to her industry.

In the country she mastered the jargon of the land and could quote fat stock prices from memory. But she never took to horses. The equestrian exuberance of her two predecessors was not for her. Females on horseback struck her as "too funny". Horsy women appealed only to her sense of the ridiculous. The rolling Cotswolds, with their yellow stone houses and rich pastures, cast a spell over her. Day excursions to London became too difficult, but in 1942 she travelled twice to Windsor, once in March for Princess Elizabeth's confirmation and in August for the christening of the Duke of Kent's youngest son Prince Michael. Three weeks later the Duke was dead, killed on active service when his warplane crashed in Scotland on its way to Iceland. The last time his mother had seen the Duke he had "looked so happy with his lovely wife [Princess Marina] & the dear baby" at Coppins. He was 39. After the funeral at St. George's Chapel, where she gazed once more upon the tomb of the Duke of Clarence, she returned to Badminton and to deaden the sorrow was soon chopping away at the ivy—"Georgie would have wished me to do so".

When at last the war ended she felt sad to leave Badminton for the treadmill of Marlborough House. She had enjoyed the free and easy life of the Cotswolds; now she must start being Queen Mary all over again. But there was work to be done. She was 78 but still active. The royal 'trade' must be carried on. The King was worn down by the demands of war, in almost startling contrast to his elder brother who, like his grandfather the Duke of Teck, had been denied any occupation suited to his abilities, although he presided over the Bahamas as governor with faultless diligence. The Duke of Windsor had all the sparkle of his grandmother Queen Alexandra, and the locust years in a sunny clime had stimulated and refreshed him. His golf was as good as ever. His mother marked the difference between her two sons when they dined together with her: she had not seen David for nine years and found him looking "very well". If the shadow of the Duchess fell between them it was banished by her merry laughter and nothing was allowed to spoil the reunion.

In the spring of 1947 the King and Queen with their daughters paid their historic state visit to South Africa, while blizzards blew Britain into the worst power shortage ever known. Queen Mary rode out the crisis with aplomb, enduring the rigours of fuel rationing with the humblest of her son's subjects. Visitors would often come upon her knitting in her suite overlooking The Mall with only a single-bar electric stove to warm the vast room. On her eightieth birthday that May she felt "tiresomely" old. Octogenarianism was a "great bore", but she enjoyed all the fuss, the pleasure of donning one of her famous rose-pink gowns glittering with tiny beads, and even made a rare speech at the family party. Her greatest pleasure that year was the betrothal of Princess Elizabeth and Prince Philip, who flew to her immediately to let "dear Grannie" admire the engagement ring, to which she added as wedding presents some jewellery from the treasury of her own marriage gifts. The wedding in November was the first royal Abbey ceremony of its kind since that of the Duke and Duchess of Kent thirteen years before, and the Queen Mother prepared herself for it with a gaiety which, as she conceded, was "not bad for eighty". Prince Charles was born in 1948, and her delight in great-grandmotherhood found expression in her gift of a silver-gilt christening cup and cover. It was 168 years old, originally presented by George III to a godson. Queen Mary thus handed down to her great-grandson a gift made by her great-grandfather five generations earlier.

But the King was ailing, and so was the Queen Mother. Sciatica forced her into inactivity; it was "all a great nuisance" having to appear in public in a wheelchair, too reminiscent of Queen Charlotte and Aunt Augusta in their declining years. By this method she toured the Festival of Britain in May 1951, but found it, as did so many others, quite ugly and a poor parody of the Great Exhibition a century earlier. Gradually she recovered, but the King's operation for lung cancer in September oppressed her; she never really believed he would survive it. His death at Sandringham on 6th February 1952 broke even her courageous spirit. From that time she fretted herself quietly to death. Four British Sovereigns and an heir to the throne had died during her lifetime and a fifth Sovereign had abdicated. Her first duty was to drive to Clarence House to kiss the hand of Queen Elizabeth II, who had broken off her Commonwealth tour in Kenya and posted back to London. Then she put on her black—how many times she had done so, and how she *hated* black clothes—and in the great Hall of Kings at Westminster she paid homage to the King, dead at the age of 56. It was her last public act. On the day of the funeral she watched the cortège pass along The Mall before settling down tearfully at her television set to watch her son pass to his tomb at Windsor.

It was the winter of her desolation. Queen Mary concentrated on matters to be settled at her death. A new will was drafted, and the dispositions she had made in favour of George VI were transferred to his daughter, the Queen. Plans for her appearance at the coronation in 1953 brightened those cheerless days. There had never been a coronation attended by a Queen Grandmother, and she took simple pleasure in the thought, even inspecting Queen Victoria's coronation robes in the the Kensington Palace museum in search of ideas for her granddaughter's regalia.

Stands were going up in the heart of London, and in early February she drove out to see the decorations. But she had a presentiment of death, and made her wish known that should she die before June the ceremony must not be postponed for the sake of Court mourning. An icy blast blew from the east when, on 9th February, Londoners saw the old Queen, erect and benign as ever, passing by in her limousine with that little hand-wave which was as well known as the standard fluttering from the masthead above the House of the Queens in The Mall. On 24th March the standard was lowered. Before she slipped into unconsciousness she had passages from a book on India read aloud to her. As she had said all those years ago, India would always be engraved upon her heart.

Parliament assembled to honour her memory while she lay in state in Westminster Hall, so soon to follow her son on the journey to Windsor. Mr. Churchill in his tailcoat frowned at the motley array of lounge suits worn by most members of the Commons. "Why don't they wear dark suits?" he inquired. Perhaps they had none, he was told, for it was only recently that clothing had been freed from wartime controls.

"But I'm sure they'd find something suitable if they *searched their wardrobes*," he protested.

It can only be surmised how Queen Mary, the most liberal-minded of the three Queen Dowagers of the present study, would have laughed at the notion that modern Members of Parliament had wardrobes large enough to be *searched*. Especially for dark clothes. She had always *hated* black.

Works Consulted

ALEXANDROV, VICTOR, *The End of the Romanovs*, Hutchinson 1966
BALDWIN, A. W., *My Father: The True Story*, George Allen and Unwin
BATTISCOMBE, GEORGINA, *Queen Alexandra*, Constable 1969
BOLITHO, HECTOR, *George VI*, Eyre and Spottiswoode 1937
BUCHAN, JOHN, *The King's Grace, 1910–1935*, University of London
  Press 1935
CHURCHILL, SIR WINSTON, *The Second World War*, Cassell 1948–54
DORAN'S *Memoirs of Queen Adelaide*, London 1861
FEILING, KEITH, *The Life of Neville Chamberlain*, Macmillan 1946
FULFORD, ROGER, *Royal Dukes*, Gerald Duckworth and Co. Ltd. 1933
GREENWOOD, ALICE DRAYTON, *Lives of the Hanoverian Queens of England*,
  G. Bell & Sons Ltd. 1911
GREVILLE *Memoirs*, ed. by H. Reeve, 4th edition, London 1875
HATCH, ALDEN, *The Mountbattens*, W. H. Allen 1966
HIBBERT, CHRISTOPHER, *The Court at Windsor*, Longmans 1964
HOPKIRK, MARY, *Queen Adelaide*, John Murray 1946
HOUSMAN, LAURENCE, *Victoria Regina: A Dramatic Biography*, Jonathan
  Cape Ltd. 1934
KEPPEL, ALICE, *Edwardian Daughter*, Hamish Hamilton 1958
LOCKHART, J. G., *Life of Cosmo Gordon Lang*, Hodder and Stoughton
MACKENZIE, COMPTON, *The Windsor Tapestry*, Chatto and Windus
MADOL, HANS ROGER, *The Private Life of Queen Alexandra*, Hutchinson
  1940
MAGNUS, PHILIP, *King Edward the Seventh*, John Murray 1964
MAGNUS, PHILIP, *Kitchener: Portrait of an Imperialist*, John Murray 1958
MALEY'S *Historical Recollections of the Reign of William IV*, London 1860
MALLET, MARIE, *Life with Queen Victoria: Letters from Court, 1887–1901*,
  John Murray 1968

MARIE LOUISE, PRINCESS, *My Memoirs of Six Reigns* (*1872–1956*), Evans Brothers 1956

MOLESWORTH'S *History of England from 1830 to 1874*, London 1874

MORTON, FREDERIC, *The Rothschilds: A Family Portrait*, Secker and Warburg 1961

NICOLSON, HAROLD, *King George V: His Life and Reign*, Constable 1952

NICOLSON, HAROLD, *Diaries and Letters*, 3 vols., 1930–39, 1939–45 and 1945–62, Collins 1966–68

POPE-HENNESSEY, JAMES, *Queen Mary 1867–1953*, George Allen and Unwin 1959

SANDARS, MARY F., *The Life and Times of Queen Adelaide*, Stanley Paul and Co. 1915

STRACHEY, LYTTON, *Queen Victoria*, Chatto and Windus 1921

TAYLOR, A. J. P., *Bismarck: The Man and the Statesman*, Hamish Hamilton Ltd. 1955

TISDALL, E. E. P., *Unpredictable Queen*, Stanley Paul and Co. Ltd. 1953

TOOLEY, *The Life of Queen Alexandra*, Hodder and Stoughton 1902

WHEELER-BENNETT, JOHN W., *King George VI: His Life and Reign*, Macmillan 1958

WILKINS, W. H., *Mrs Fitzherbert and George IV*, Mellifont Press

WINDSOR, HRH THE DUKE OF, K.G., *A King's Story: Memoirs*, Cassell 1951

WOODWARD, KATHLEEN, *Queen Mary*, Hutchinson 1927

Index

—— Sir Henry, 93
—— General Sir William, 104
Konitz, Freiherr von, 33
Kruger, President Paul, 128

L
Laeken, Palace, 103
'Lancaster, Countess of' (incognito of Queen Adelaide and Queen Victoria), 70
Lancet, The, 112, 119
Lang, Archbishop Cosmo, 185
Langara, Don Juan de, 31
Langtry, Lillie, 118
Lawrence, Miss Susan, 177
Leiningen, Prince Emich of, 27
Leinster, Duchess of, 120
Leopold, King of the Belgians, 22–3, 32, 55, 72–3, 77, 102–3, 105
—— Prince, Duke of Albany, 109, 182
Lieven, Princess de, 46–7, 50, 62–3, 71
Lind, Jenny, 108
Lipton, Sir Thomas, 129
Liverpool, Lord, 36, 40, 45
Lloyd George, 1st Earl, 136, 151
London, Duke of (title), 161
London Bridge, 57
London Hospital, 113
Londonderry, 3rd Marquess of, 72
—— 6th Marchioness of, 120
Longair, Sir William, 94
Lords, House of, 32, 48, 60 *et seq.*, 84
Louis XVI, King of France, 64, 67
Louis XVIII, King of France, 34
Louise Eleanora, Grand Duchess of Saxe-Coburg-Meiningen, 17, 27 *et seq.*, 38, 73, 78
Louise of Hesse-Cassel, Queen of Denmark, 92, 96 *et seq.*, 101–4, 111; death, 128
Louise, Princess Royal, *see* Fife, Princess Royal (Louise), Duchess of
Louise of Saxe-Weimar, Princess, 44, 59, 68–70, 78
Louise of Sweden, Princess, 111
Louis Napoleon, Prince Imperial of the French, 116, 118
Louis Philippe, King of France, 59, 77
Ludwig, Emil, 124–5
Luton Hoo, 158–9
Lyndhurst, Lord, 72

M
Macarthur, Miss Mary, 177 *et seq.*
Macclesfield, Lady, 110
MacDonald, J. Ramsay, 183–4
Mackenzie, Sir Morell, 123
Madeira, 76
Magnus, Sir Philip, 125
Mallet, Marie, 124, 128–9, 130
Malmesbury, 1st Earl of, 35
Malta, 75, 172
Man, Isle of, 87
Manchester, Duchess of, 115
Margaret, Queen of Sweden, 151
—— Princess, Countess of Snowdon, 182, 187
Margate, 106
Maria, Queen of Portugal, 69, 70
Marie Antoinette, Queen of France, 45, 60, 64, 67
Marie Feodorovna (Dagmar), Empress of Russia, 89, 95, 97–8, 102, 105–7, 111; accession, 121–2; 127–8, 133 *et seq.*, 150, 160
Marie Louise, Princess, 87
'Marlbocracy, The', 114–15, 118, 129, 131, 165, 168
Marlborough, HMS, 136
Marlborough House, 56, 74, 76, 78, 84, 98, 105, 110, 112, 114, 117–18, 123, 131, 133–4, 136 *et seq.*, 153, 168, 170, 173, 186–9, 191–3
Mary, Queen, 11–13; birth, 143–4, 152–153, 157 *et seq.*; her family, 144 *et seq.*, 151 *et seq.*, 164–6; engagement to Duke of Clarence, 126, 148, 159; engagement to George V, 148, 160 *et seq.*; marriage, 127, 162–3; married life, 169 *et seq.*; her children, 164 *et seq.*, 169, 170 *et seq.*, 185 *et seq.*; parents-in-law, 138–9, 150, 168, 173; Queen Victoria, 143–4, 153; as Princess of Wales, 167 *et seq.*; accession, 133, 149, 150, 171 *et seq.*; coronation, 150, 172; state visit to Berlin, 151, 176; state visit to France, 151, 176; women's rights and labour problems, 150, 158, 173 *et seq.*, 176 *et seq.*, 183; state visit to Ireland, 166; overseas visits, 167 *et seq.*; and India, 171, 174–5; 1914–18 war, 176 *et seq.*; 1939–45 war, 188–91; silver wedding, 179, 180; Silver Jubilee, 184; death of George V, 184; as Queen Mother,